JAYDEN DANIELS

SMOOTH OPERATOR

20

COMMANDERS
5

To my grandchildren Oliver, Hadley, Autumn and Leo.
May you grow up to be Commanders fans.

This book is available in quantity at special discounts for your group or organization.

For further information, contact:

Triumph Books LLC
814 North Franklin Street
Chicago, Illinois 60610
Phone: (312) 337-0747
www.triumphbooks.com

Printed in U.S.A.
ISBN: 978-1-63727-986-1

Content packaged by Mojo Media, Inc.
Joe Funk: Editor
Jason Hinman: Creative Director

Front and Back Cover Photos by AP Images.

CONTENTS

DANIELS
1

THE ARRIVAL

'WHY NOT JAYDEN?'

Once Commanders Zeroed in on Drafting Jayden Daniels, It Was Full Speed Ahead

It was not a straight line to Jayden Daniels.

The Washington Commanders took the long way, lingered over several junctures and met regularly over who the team would select with the second pick in the 2024 NFL Draft. What seems like a no-brainer in hindsight still took a village to decide. But once the team decided on Daniels, they sprinted right to him.

"Why not Jayden?" said general manager Adam Peters not long after the draft. "To us, he was special in every way on the field, off the field...I turned on Jayden [college games] for the first time here and I couldn't believe it. I honestly couldn't believe how good he was. Just the way he could process, the way he could see the field, go through reads, deliver on time, deliver with pressure in his face, take a hot and deliver a third down pass and move the chains. He's the best deep ball thrower we thought in the draft.

"And that's even before we started watching him run. And the way he runs, we talk about it kind of takes your soul as a defense. You think you got him and then, all of a sudden, he runs off a 40-yard run and this is against the SEC. This isn't against lower competition. This is against the best of the best.

"We knew it was Jayden for a while and it would have taken a lot for it not to be Jayden. The whole building was in."

It seems an easy pick now. Chicago was taking Caleb Williams of Southern California with the first selection. Commanders new offensive coordinator Kliff Kingsbury just spent the past season working directly with Williams at USC. If Kingsbury wasn't standing on a draft table ready pleading for someone he just mentored, then not trading up for Williams was an easy pass.

Still, there was a growing consensus on several quarterbacks to consider. Aside Daniels, Drake Maye of North Carolina, Michael Penix of Washington and J.J. McCarthy of Michigan were highly rated.

Each offered different strengths. Maye would be drafted third by New England and started 12 games with a solid 88.1 pass rating. Penix was taken eighth and started three games with mixed

Jayden Daniels greets NFL commissioner Roger Goodell after being selected second overall in the 2024 NFL Draft out of LSU.

results. McCarthy was chosen 10th by Minnesota before missing the season with a knee injury.

Meanwhile, Daniels won a record 10 Offensive Player of the Week awards en route to Offensive Rookie of the Year. He earned 48 of 49 votes. It was that convincing.

Daniels spoke on draft night with his trademark maturity that fans soon realized was the passer's personal style. To Daniels, there is no I in team nor an M and E, either.

"A competitor, a leader," he described as his traits, "but someone that just wants to win at all costs and help the team win no matter what because it's team first always.

"I'm just coming to compete . . . and really trying to play my role, whatever that is. I just want to be the best teammate to help the team win and we can bring back to victories to D.C, to the DMV and have some fun."

The Commanders research dated back five years on Daniels when Doug Williams met the passer at Arizona State. Williams was speaking at a seminar for Black quarterbacks. The two became fast friends. Williams didn't forget that relationship as the team prepared for the 2024 draft.

Peters benefited greatly from Williams' intel. Peters didn't scout quarterbacks before named Washington's general manager on Jan. 15. Instead, he was scouting the back end of the draft while working as San Francisco 49ers' assistant GM.

It would take a lot of catching up to suddenly worry over the No. 2 pick versus late rounders. But then, Peters became well known for San Francisco choosing Brock Purdy with the final pick of the 2022 draft. "Mr. Irrelevant" went from third stringer to 5-0 and leading the 49ers during a 10-game winning streak all the way to the NFC Championship.

No one doubted Peters could make a franchise-defining pick, but due diligence is the foundation of his decision-making process.

"We did a lot of work on Jayden," Peters said. "In terms of every single person we spoke to, it was just exemplary as a person, personal character, football character, his work ethic his football intelligence, how much he cared, his leadership, how he is as a teammate. We went back to high school."

The Commanders spoke to Arizona coach Herm Edwards where Daniels spent 2019-21. Daniels was a prized recruit, having started playing flag football at age 5. He moved to tackle football two years later when a short stint at cornerback soon gave way to quarterback. It was then Daniels acquired his cool demeanor after his father Jay Daniels said there was no crying in football.

A versatile athlete who played soccer and basketball, Daniels made varsity football as a freshman at Cajon High School in San Bernardino, Calif. in 2015. But he first needed a doctor's approval after weighing just 125 pounds. Still, Daniels led Cajon to the state semifinals. Daniels broke his finger in the 2016 opener but still played all season. By 2017, Daniels set California record for more than 6,400 passing yards while taking Cajon to the state Division 2-AA finals. Cajon reached the state Division 3 championship in Daniels' senior season.

The 2024 NFL Draft launched a bright new era for the Commanders with Jayden Daniels at the helm.

OrthoVirginia
OrthoVirginia
DANIELS
1

Overall, Daniels played 53 high school games with 210 touchdowns and more than 17,600 passing yards. The four-star prospect received 25 college scholarship offers before accepting Arizona State. Indeed, he graduate high school early and arrived at ASU in January 2019.

Naturally, Daniels was ASU's starter as a freshman. Despite a knee injury, he set a Sun Devils freshman record for passing yards and named Most Valuable Player in the Sun Bowl victory over Florida State.

The team played only four games in 2020 because of the COVID pandemic. After his third season when leading ASU to the Las Vegas Bowl, Daniels transferred to LSU after Arizona State coaches left over an NCAA investigation regarding recruiting violations.

Daniels became LSU's starter for 2022, leading the Tigers to the SEC Championship final. As a senior in 2023, Daniels became the first passer in Football Bowl Subdivision history to pass for 250 yards and run for 200 against Florida. He threw eight touchdown passes against Georgia State.

Overall, Daniels finished with 40 touchdowns passing, 10 rushing and nearly 5,000 total yards. He won the Heisman Trophy and finished with 16,000 total yards in 55 college games with a 37-18 record.

Peters talked to LSU head coach Brian Kelly, but the key interview was with director of player retention Sherman Wilson, who worked with Daniels daily. The passer remembers their relationship as tough love that made him better.

"[Wilson} was there with me every day, 5 a.m., late nights," Daniels said. "He pushed me. He challenged me. He's like a big brother to me. We'd argue, we didn't see eye to eye, but he wanted the best for me. He's seen something in me that I ain't see in myself. He helped me bring it out for sure."

Daniels also remembers his days at LSU as instrumental to handling adult responsibilities. A self-described introvert with a close relationship with his family, Daniels needed to learn independence while playing half a country away from his California home.

"I would say I got more comfortable when I was in Louisiana," he said. "I was older. Obviously, it's a life I want to live, but when I first came out of high school, I would've been homesick. I couldn't go too far from home. But once I made that transition to Louisiana, it helped me grow even more. Being out there on my own, I wasn't really dependent on my family. More so you know how to figure some stuff out, who I want to be as a person, as a man."

Now a Commander, Daniels' first task was his jersey number. Daniels always wore No. 5 for his favorite boyhood heroes Donovan McNabb and Reggie Bush. However, punter Tress Way had worn No, 5 since 2014.

A multiple Pro Bowler, Way could have kept the number, but surrendered it without financial remuneration when feeling Daniels would be so vital to the team. Way instead chose No. 10.

Way knew the future now belonged to a different No. 5. ■

Head coach Dan Quinn, Jayden Daniels and general manager Adam Peters are all smiles at the press conference officially introducing Daniels as a Commander.

THE LONG ROAD TO JAYDEN

The QB Landscape in DC Wasn't Pretty Before Finding Jayden Daniels

Garrett Gilbert was literally the last man standing.

The NFL even gave the Washington Football Team an extra day to get healthy during the 2021 COVID pandemic and let the franchise play on a Tuesday for the first time ever. Still, Washington quarterbacks Taylor Heinicke or Josh Allen couldn't pass a health check hours before the game.

So just four days after signing with Washington and only one career start, Gilbert opened against the Philadelphia Eagles. It was even a respectable effort in the loss. Gilbert never played again.

Such stories like Gilbert and nearly three dozen other passers explain why Commanders fans went nuts when drafting Jayden Daniels second overall in 2024.

Not that Washington hadn't tried to draft a franchise passer before. Robert Griffin III was nicknamed "Black Jesus" by teammates even before his first 2012 training camp practice. Griffin led the team to the playoffs as a rookie before suffering a career-altering injury in the postseason.

Washington also drafted Heath Shuler (third overall in 1994), Patrick Ramsey (32nd in 2002), Jason Campbell (25th in 2005) and Dwayne Haskins (15th in 2019) in the first round. Campbell was the only decent one and lasted just four years.

Shuler could never find linebackers, including his own in practice. After yet another interception during a midweek workout, linebacker Marvcus Patton was so frustrated that he gave Shuler a black eye.

Coach Steve Spurrier told owner Dan Snyder the latter could draft Ramsey, but "Ball Coach" wouldn't play him. Still, none of Spurrier's preferred passers succeeded so Ramsey went 10-14 under Spurrier and successor Jim Zorn.

Coach Jay Gruden said Snyder got off his yacht and ordered the team to draft Haskins, who was a high school friend of the owner's son. Haskins loved filming workouts in parks, but with

Washington football legend Mark Rypien set the standard at quarterback for the franchise with few finding lasting success in the decades since.

AISE HAIL
Raise Hail
11

Ranking 35 starters since Washington won its last Super Bowl championship in 1991.

Player	Years	Record	Comment
Jayden Daniels	2024-	14-6	10-time Rookie of Week
Mark Rypien	1988-93	45-27	Was Super Bowl MVP
Kirk Cousins	2012-17	26-30-1	Three 4,000+-yard seasons
Brad Johnson	1999-2000	17-10	Won a playoff game
Alex Smith	2018, 2020	11-5	Gruesome leg injury
Trent Green	1997-98	6-8	Too costly to re-sign
Jason Campbell	2006-09	20-32	New OC every year
Robert Griffin III	2012-14	14-21	Rookie injury ruined career
Gus Frerotte	1994-98	19-26-1	7th-rounder flashed occasionally
Mark Brunell	2004-06	15-18	Gibbs wanted old vet
Taylor Heinicke	2020-22	12-11-1	Street free agent was a baller
Rich Gannon	1993	1-3	One-year stopgap
Sam Howell	2022-23	5-13	Gutsy 5th round pick led NFL in INTs
Rex Grossman	2010-11	6-10	"Sexy" once threw five picks
Colt McCoy	2014-18	1-6	Hurt when given chance
Donovan McNabb	2010	5-8	Such a bad fit
Tony Banks	2001	8-6	Surprise one-shot passer
Jeff Hostetler	1997	2-1	One last check before retirement
Carson Wentz	2022	2-5	Opening day starter fell quickly
Heath Shuler	1994-96	4-9	Never saw linebackers
Jeff George	2000-01	1-6	Called "Coach killer" for a reason
Patrick Ramsey	2002-05	10-14	Out of sync with coaches
John Friesz	1994	1-3	Just another arm
Todd Collins	2007, 2009	3-0	Strangest W/L of all
Shane Matthews	2002	3-4	Ball Coach loved him
Garrett Gilbert	2021	0-1	COVID game spot starter
Tim Hasselbeck	2003	1-4	Was next man up
Cary Conklin	1992-93	0-2	Threw five touchdowns
Josh Johnson	2018	1-2	Only career win in nine seasons
Case Keenum	2019	1-7	Started bad, finished worse
Danny Wuerffel	2002	2-2	Best of "Ball Coach" trio
Dwayne Haskins	2019-20	3-10	Drafted by owner, not staff
Ryan Fitzpatrick	2021	0-1	Hurt after 20 minutes
Mark Sanchez	2018	0-1	Emergency signing
John Beck	2011	0-3	Nice guy finished last

a stadium of people watching went 3-10 in less than two seasons before cut. Haskins died less than two years later when struck by a truck while running across a Miami highway.

Sadly, those five first-rounders were the highlights among 35 starters over 33 years. Oh, there were some good quarterbacks to pass through. Brad Johnson led Washington to the playoffs. Trent Green, Gus Frerotte, Kirk Cousins and Alex Smith saw some short-term success.

And then there was Rex Grossman throwing five interceptions only because he couldn't throw six. Josh Johnson winning his only career game. Mark Brunell arriving on the downside of his career. Ryan Fitzpatrick suffering a career-ending injury just 20 minutes into the first game. Todd Collins making fans wish they were drinking a Tom Collins.

Commanders coach Dan Quinn tried to be openly patient with Daniels, making him earn the job without the obvious wink-wink over media questions of how the rookie was doing. It was the worst-kept secret in a nation's capital believed to have more than 10,000 spies.

Everyone knew Daniels would mark the seventh straight year of a different opening-day passer. They just hoped he would be more than that.

"I definitely understand our fan base has been waiting for the franchise QB," Quinn said, "but I also don't want Jayden feeling any ghosts. I don't want any comparison or any of that other stuff. I think it was a Teddy Roosevelt quote, 'Comparison is the thief of joy.'"

Daniels didn't get caught in the hype, either. He remained modest every day of the season, even after some remarkable performances that earned him a record 10 Rookie of the Week belts that overflowed a box in his garage. One day Daniels will mount them on a wall, but that day will come years from now.

"I don't feel no pressure," he said. "I'm just going to come in and just be me."

Said Quinn: "I agree with Jayden on that. And I don't want to compare him to anybody but him because he is still growing. I can't wait to see who he's becoming."

After earning NFL Offensive Player of the Year, Daniels is clearly the team's best quarterback since Sonny Jurgensen in the 1960s. And, Jurgensen is considered the team's best passer since World War II, though Jurgensen always claims fellow Pro Football Hall of Famer Sammy Baugh (1937-52) was better.

Still, Washington has come a long way since signing street free agents as starters. ■

FIRST EMBRACE

While Jayden Daniels Technically Had to Compete for the Job, Early Returns Made Starting Spot a Formality

Jayden Daniels was drafted to be the face of the franchise. It wasn't a free pass to the huddle, though.

Coach Dan Quinn wanted Daniels to earn his starting role to bolster respect among veterans knowing the rookie deserved the job over veteran Marcus Mariota. Daniels wanted to earn it for the same reason.

It began on the field just a week after the draft. The rookie camp saw Daniels take to the Ashburn, Va. complex like he had been there for years. Daniels found quick chemistry with fellow draftee receiver Luke McCaffrey in early-morning walkthroughs before others arrived. It continued in the afternoons when Daniels processed new plays.

"I like competing," Daniels said. "Regardless, if I was announced the starter or not, you still got to compete. You still can't be content of your job. It is your job to seal the deal.

"God put me in this place for a reason. My life is already written out. He got a plan. I'm just following it. But that comes with the work. At the end of the day, nothing is given to me. I've got to put in the work. I've got to learn the playbook, earn the respect of my teammates and go out there and try to win football games."

What most amazed coaches was Daniels' quick grasp of the playbook, which is usually the size of a small book. He used virtual reality for quicker processing, though Daniels still walked through the plays at dawn and later in afternoons.

"[Daniels] has a plan for studying," said offensive coordinator Kliff Kingsbury. "He has a plan for practice. He has a plan for watching film. He knows what he wants to be and where he wants to go. To be that young and coming in here with that mindset is really encouraging."

Coach Dan Quinn immediately knew Washington chose the right passer based on body language and temperament alone.

"[Daniels has] the humility and the hard work of the rookie with a little bit of swag of an older guy," Quinn said. "That's a pretty nice blend to have."

Washington spent the next month in OTAs and minicamp with Daniels ramping up. The most encouraging sign – the ball was rarely on

Jayden Daniels speaks with the media during his first days on the field as a Commander at rookie minicamp in May 2024.

NW
NORTHWEST
FEDERAL CREDIT UNION

AYDEN DANIELS
OAKLEY
COMMANDERS
NW
NORTHWEST
FEDERAL CREDIT UNION
EQUIPMENT
NFL

the ground. Daniels' accuracy was remarkable no matter if the play was short or long, a simple drill or 11 on 11s.

Daniels was ready when training camp opened in late July. He'd spent the month-long break since minicamp studying the playbook and throwing to receivers.

"My experience with young quarterbacks [is] like Quinn says, 'It's not one size fits all' and I think everybody can see what's happening," said general manager Adam Peters. "You don't want to slow it down. You want to let it happen naturally."

Quinn held to his pledge of competition when the preseason began, laying out his levels of comparison between Daniels and Mariota with third-stringer Jeff Driskel having a good summer, too. Daniels absorbed every play, big and small.

"When there's shots down the field, what takes place on those," Quinn said. "We haven't had a lot of those because of our intentional work down in the red zone first."

Still, it didn't take long to decide. Daniels was named the starter on Aug. 19. A sharp practice against Miami earlier showed Daniels' readiness.

"The command of it, the accuracy, the details of it," Quinn said. "That was one of the best practices I'd seen him have. I think that was more in line with who he is, what he does, the checks, the calls, the communication, the delivery of the ball. It was just cool to see all of that come to life."

Quinn was also watching veteran reaction to Daniels to see if they were willing followers.

"What Jayden got across is, I put the work in," Quinn said. "He's demonstrated to his teammates over and over again is, 'Man, you can count on me. I'll make the right call, put us in the right play, make the right decisions.'"

Daniels felt veterans always gave him a fair chance rather than dismiss a first-year player. A huddle must silently respect the quarterback, or those critical few seconds become chaotic with others voicing opinions.

"I don't think they necessarily treat me as a rookie," Daniels said. "The day I got here, everybody was treated equally."

Mariota knew his likely role was backup and mentor to Daniels. The elder passer appreciated the respect given by open competition, but Mariota saw something special in Daniels from the start of training camp, so the outcome wasn't surprising. Mariota mostly encouraged Daniels to be himself and not feel pressured to do what didn't come naturally.

"When you're a young guy," Mariota said, "you really want to try to come in and be perfect and that's hard. I really think that can be detrimental in some sense to your growth. You're going to fail. You're going to have mistakes. What you have to be able to do is learn from your mistakes."

Now named the starter, Daniels' regimen and temperament saw no change. He was still the confident newcomer trying to fit in rather than be the anointed leader.

"Everything in my life is you gotta earn it. Nothing's given," he said. "You gotta earn your right to stay...What I did in college doesn't matter."

But what Daniels was about to do would matter greatly. ■

While still months away from game competition, Jayden Daniels quickly looked the part during his early Washington tenure.

PATH TO IMPROVEMENT

The Willingness to Learn Made All the Difference in Early NFL Days for Jayden Daniels

The best college quarterbacks reach the NFL suddenly realizing they know nothing.

That's right – the process begins anew. For those quickly embracing not only a new offensive system, but a heightened speed of the game, success is possible. But too many passers while facing better competition, older players with more experience and often coaches forcing a system on rookies that's opposite their skillset quickly find failure.

Basically, chances of first-round quarterbacks succeeding are 50/50 at best.

How did Jayden Daniels not only succeed, but thrive?

He came ready to learn.

"I would say the speed of everything is at the front of any rookie," said coach Dan Quinn before training camp. "It's just a jump that naturally happens. Some of the windows to throw to are tighter, maybe, than they have been accustomed to based on college or how fast things go. But, by and large, those are the things you just keep improving at because now it'll eventually slow down as well. When that process happens, that's when you see a lot of the guys really take off."

The Commanders staff was filled with former quarterbacks to make Daniels' transition easier. Offensive coordinator Kliff Kingsbury was a solid college quarterback who hired fellow passers in passing game coordinator Brian Johnson, quarterbacks coach Tavita Pritchard and assistant quarterback coach David Blough, who was especially tight with Daniels.

Kingsbury said Daniels handled every step in the process well.

"I love the process," Kingsbury said. "I love how he approaches every day. How he handles the good, the bad, all the installs. He must study [the playbook] like crazy at night because every morning when we get here and he walks through with us he nails it…That's all you can ask from a young player.

"He wants more knowledge. He wants the answers. He wants to know why. If he sees something on the field, he can come back to you and tell you exactly what he saw and you can get

Jayden Daniels poses with his mother, Regina Jackson, as he makes his first appearance as an NFL franchise quarterback in the making.

OrthoVirginia
DANIELS
1

NW
NORTHWEST
5

really good information, which is a special trait for a quarterback."

Early in offseason camps, there was an emphasis for Daniels not to rely on his elusiveness regularly to lessen chances of injury. Not that Washington didn't want Daniels to run. Some teams would have turned Daniels into a statue, but Washington knew a big part of Daniels' success comes while on the run. Why diminish his chances of success? They just wanted him to be smarter and work the sidelined more than take hits in the middle of the field.

"You do want to be able to have the dual threat," said Quinn as camp opened. "It's the finish of the play if [Daniels] extends it because you're extending, usually, to remain a passer first. That's where his strength comes in. If he just gets outside the pocket to run, that's a lot easier to do. You're outside the pocket, but this player can stay alive and throw on the move. As he gets closer to contact, we're going to go over to visit with the [Washington] Nationals a lot and learn sliding and other important topics down the line."

With Daniels often running at least a handful of times per game, the Commanders also worked on protecting the ball.

"[Daniels] takes a lot of pride in that," Quinn said. "He takes a lot of pride in playing the game the right way, knowing the protections, knowing where his hots are, knowing where his dirty throwaways are when it's not there and not taking sacks, and that's a big part of his game.

"I don't remember how many interceptions he threw last year at LSU, [four versus 40 touchdowns] but it wasn't many and he was playing at a high level and a great conference. I have a great appreciation for that and as a young guy that's paramount. It's not always gonna go great, but if you can not turn the ball over and not take sacks on first, second down, you're gonna give your team a chance in most games."

Daniels' field vision was also an ongoing process. He started using virtual reality at LSU in 2023. Designed by German developer Cognilize, the VR uses custom game plans to adjust for opposing defenders speed along with road venues.

Earlier in the season, Daniels sometimes didn't see second and third receivers while on the run. Instead, there were many underneath passes when a deeper receiver was open. Daniels improved greatly over the season.

"I thought that was strong going in," Quinn said. "Where you saw the connection with him and the receivers from LSU and you heard about the work that they put in together to achieve that kind of success throwing the ball. All the different layers of throws, deep balls, crossers, out of the backfield, all of those matter and you work on all of them at different times.

"And then the decision-making process, that's a whole different part of it. 'This coverage goes to here, this look goes to here, I got a matchup I want, I go to here.' So, there's your skill work and then the processing work and the processing part for him has been excellent."

NFL teams install new plays weekly particular to the opponent. Daniels saw them

With the NFL Draft behind him, Jayden Daniels quickly got to work in anticipation of the 2024-25 NFL season.

COMMANDERS
OAKLEY
NW
NORTHWEST

each Wednesday morning before practice and worked with the plays for three days. Sometimes they were used, sometimes not after seeing how Daniels handled them.

"We keep pushing the limit with him day in, day out with these installs," Quinn said. "And it's not like it's a ton of repeat. I mean, you'll dress things up and have the same concept but run it a different way, different personnel group and he handles it really well. Whatever we've thrown at him, he's handled it and hasn't blinked and that's encouraging. We wanna make sure we don't try to overload him. We wanna allow him to use his natural gifts, and play fast, and be attacking, and confident in what he does. But so far he's handled everything with flying colors."

By opening day against Tampa Bay, Kingsbury knew he could trust Daniels enough for the latter to improvise if seeing a problem approaching the line.

"We will give [Daniels] some free reign out there at times," Kingsbury said. "If he sees good looks that he wants to get into, we'll let him attack and that's how he played at LSU. And we like that attacking mindset. Like if we get the look, let's go after it."

One month into the season, Daniels learned how to better time passes to receivers heavily covered.

"I just think that comes with the nature of playing quarterback at this league," he said. "Guys aren't open. You got to throw to some guys open and there's [defenders] that have played in this league a long time that are very savvy and know what's coming. So you got to make some tight window throws."

By midseason, Daniels was seeing NFC East opponents for the second time. That was another challenge.

"It's always difficult," Kingsbury said. "You know each other really well at that point. You have a lot of intel and you've seen each other on the field. To me, it's about not trying to do too much and stay within yourself and execute at a high level."

The one thing many teammates and coaches often mentioned of Daniels by season's end was his constantly spreading credit around the huddle. That's especially important to offensive linemen who mostly work in anonymity. Some passers just think it's all about them. When Jeff George laid on the ground after a sack in 2000, none of his linemen offered to help him up.

"[Daniels] defers credit to everybody else," Kingsbury said, "and it's all about trying to get better the next week. That's been awesome to see, but not surprising."

Ironically, Daniels success arose from failure. His very first minicamp pass sailed high above the target. The nerves showed, but he then completed several passes and the inaugural throw was forgotten...sorta.

"We will certainly keep that [tape] in our back pocket," joked Quinn. ■

The training camp work put in by Jayden Daniels would pay off in a big way during his memorable rookie season.

MEMBERS OF THE SAME CLUB

Veteran Marcus Mariota Share Similar Journey, Bond in the Washington QB Room

Jayden Daniels was ecstatic. He was running around, leaping with joy. Washington just finished the season beating Dallas with a walk-off touchdown catch by Terry McLaurin and Daniels had nothing to do with it.

Marcus Mariota threw that pass.

"The most emotional I've seen [Daniels] is his joy for Marcus in that spot," said coach Dan Quinn. "When Marcus threw the game-winning touchdown in Dallas, [Daniels] was the most emotional. Where he's the one in charge, he's iced up man. Inside the lens of that helmet, he's a killer."

Mariota and Daniels aren't typical allies despite similarities. Sure, they're both Heisman Trophy winners and No. 2 overall picks. That's an elite club.

But they're also a decade apart in age and Mariota could have easily seen Daniels as a threat to probably the former's last chance to start in the NFL. Instead, Mariota became a mentor, unofficial assistant coach and role player who finished with the second-best quarterback rating of his career.

"Me and Marcus kind of got a similar story," Daniels said. "He kind of felt like he had to wear the cape and stuff like that. He's just given me his experience through his time through the league, his knowledge and he's been instrumental in my development. Without him, I wouldn't be in this position."

Mariota's uneven career is far from a bust. Tennessee gave him more than four seasons before benching him in 2019 with a 29-32 record. Mariota eked out three straight winning seasons at 8-7, 9-6 and 7-6 from 2016-18, but the stats were ugly. His quarterback rating was always in the 50s, about half of the league's elite passers.

Finally, Mariota moved on to Las Vegas in 2020 with no decisions in two seasons. He only threw two passes in the second year. Atlanta gave Mariota a second chance in 2022 before pulling him after a 5-8 start. Mariota spent 2023 mopping

The bond between Jayden Daniels and Marcus Mariota began to form during training camp, a sign of things to come.

up three games in Philadelphia before signing one-year deal with Washington that went so well he re-upped for 2025.

Mariota only played in three games for Washington with no starts despite nearly doing so once after Daniels missed midweek practices with bruised ribs. His final stat line was completing 34 of 44 passes for 364 yards and four touchdowns for an 87.8 rating.

"This game humbles you," Mariota said. "I was humbled very early on in my career in Tennessee, [but] I just love ball. I love being around it."

Coaches appreciated Mariota's humble attitude when many veterans would have soured.

"[Mariota has] been open and honest and just phenomenal," said offensive coordinator Kliff Kingsbury. "I can't say enough good things. . . . He is revered in the building because of his work ethic and the way he treats people and his ability. I don't think you can put a value on that."

But the benefits to Daniels are immeasurable. The rookie posed so many questions to his elder.

"Just how to handle adversity, that thing that you go through," Daniels said. "You're going to have ups and downs throughout the season so how do you deal with that? How do you prepare for a short week? How do you prepare for a week 14 bye and stuff like that. How do you manage your body throughout the season."

Coaches exhaled when seeing Daniels respond to Mariota's advice both on the field and in the classroom. It's one thing for coaches to teach or critique but coming from a teammate means so much more.

"Just encouragement, I would say, is the thing that you see," Quinn said. "And so, 'What'd you see? How'd it go back?' So, I wouldn't say coaching one another, but giving support to one another and what could happen, 'What's next?'

"Seeing those two things take place is always good because, whether you're a veteran or a rookie, having somebody look there and watch and just give you feedback peer to peer, that helps. When it comes from your teammate, that's a big deal."

Said Mariota: "When you have a guy that's willing to learn, that wants to absorb as much knowledge as he can, I think that makes the whole room better."

Sliding, of all things, was a key teachable moment. Daniels really didn't know how to slide much like predecessor Robert Griffin in 2012. The difference is Griffin never listened or learned. Mariota is an excellent slider and Daniels became proficient by late season. Sliding is vital because it signals intent to forgo more yards and prevents defenders from taking cheap shots.

"What's awesome is having Marcus Mariota, who was a similar talent with his legs coming in," Kingsbury said. "He had to learn when to get down. When to surrender when the party's over. And to have a guy like that with his knowledge helping Jayden through this deal has been really special for all of us. It's a little better advice coming from Marcus."

While Jayden Daniels emerged from training camp as the clear starter at quarterback for the Commanders, the tight knit position group would go on to help his development along the way.

Spotting an opposing "spy" player that concentrates just on the opposing quarterback rather than the play itself is another talent Daniels needed to better learn.

"You can figure that out about the first time they run it," Kingsbury said. "If they want to burn one just spying him then somebody's going to be open on the back end."

Ultimately, Mariota helped Daniels gain respect in the locker room. Veterans often don't like following rookies. They want a ready-made player at the most important position. But, players also recognize the value of a special talent like Daniels so they're more patient. Mariota told Daniels hard work would be seen by teammates and gain their respect even before game accomplishments.

"I think that's very important in the quarterback position to stand in front of these guys," Mariota said, "especially older players and kind of nail it and say, 'I got this. I got it figured out.' He's done a great job of that."

Mariota returned for 2025 knowing Daniels is firmly the starter. The passer loves the game so much he's willing to probably finish his career as a mentor. As long as Daniels is willing to listen, Mariota seems willing to teach. ■

SEASON OPENING STRUGGLE

Jayden Daniels Flashes Skills, Gets NFL Reality Check in Debut Loss

It wasn't the start the Commanders and Jayden Daniels envisioned. Actually, it was quite the opposite.

The Tampa Bay Buccaneers dominated Washington in the season opener, 37-20. Washington never led. Never came close to leading. The debut of coach Dan Quinn looked unpolished after playing regulars little over the preseason. Maybe a team with 60 percent roster turnover needed more time together.

"You need the struggle to see the identity develop," Quinn said. "You don't want it, but you do need it. That part is hard, and that struggle happened tonight. So we'll take these lessons, and we'll work on them."

With no real expectations on the season after 4-13 in 2023, the Commanders had the luxury of time. That said, Quinn and general manager Adam Peters were seething after the loss. Nobody told them it's OK to lose in a rebuilding season. They considered it a reloading year and didn't like firing blanks.

But, really, all eyes were on Daniels because he was the cornerstone of turning around the franchise. And, it was a decent effort in defeat.

Daniels completed 17 of 24 passes for 184 yards and a 93.1 rating versus a solid defense. But it was Daniels' running that was somewhat surprising. After teamwide talking for months over not relying on his legs, Daniels ran 16 times for 88 yards and two touchdowns.

Moving chains and scoring is never a bad thing. It's just not often sustainable because of potential injuries so Commanders coaches and players were a little reserved in their reviews.

"I thought he got to fully express all the things that he has of using his legs," Quinn said, "you know, being aggressive down the field... But what I can tell you is we got one hell of a competitor in him. We're just getting started with him and the guys."

Daniels thought he did fair but didn't want to be jubilant after losing. As the season progressed, that was pretty much the passer's style.

Jayden Daniels was solid in his NFL debut, but the Commanders got an early season wakeup call with a 37-20 loss to the Buccaneers.

COMMANDERS
5

"I grade myself hard. We didn't win. I'm a competitor. I like to win, but overall it went well, pretty well," he said. "There's some stuff that as an offense we left on the field. We have to execute better, but it's a long season. We're going to move on from this."

The room wasn't too big for Daniels in his much-anticipated debut after chosen second overall in the draft five months earlier. All the preparation was focused on the opener with the contingency that it was a long season. No one but Daniels expected a monster effort, so Quinn met with the rookie beforehand to ensure the latter didn't come out of the tunnel wearing a cape.

"This is a cool customer, man," Quinn said. "And you're always looking to see the next marker. And that's why we were so intentional about what we did during training camp to hit all the marks along the way, and [it's] no different than this. This is another step for him to go.

"Having that confidence to play well oftentimes comes from the preparation. You can't wait for this game because you put the work in to go, and Jayden falls under that category."

Daniels admitted feeling butterflies before the game. Yet, he was concentrating on the game and not the glory.

"Once that ball is kicked and I run on the field, take a deep breath, be where your feet are and go play football," he said. "It's the same game I've been playing since I was a kid. Even though the stakes are higher, I still revert back to the time where I was 7 years old playing against my friends."

Daniels' biggest run was a 17-yarder. He would average running nearly 60 percent on the right side over the season and the opener showed his ability to look for the pass and then tuck and run. There were a couple of scary moments when Daniels' helmet popped off, too.

"When the chances were there for him to go, I thought he really nailed it," Daniels said. "That said, like, in the game he was exactly the same as back in Ashburn [practices.] Confident, strong, clear-eyed about how to go attack, going down to the end. How about this play? He was just thinking and processing quickly."

Teammates were closely watching Daniels, too. It was the seventh straight year Washington started a different passer on opening day and everyone wondered if this time would be the beginning of a new age.

"I think, for the first time, there was a lot of stuff thrown at him," guard Sam Cosmi said, "and for the most part, I think his ability to stay calm amongst adversity was very strong. I didn't feel from him anything wavering or any panic or anything like that.

"There was a moment at the very end - we were in the huddle during like a timeout - and we kind of just looked at each other like, 'Hey man, we [have] something here. It is a two-minute drive - we can do something. Let's learn from this.'"

Receiver Terry McLaurin wasn't his usual dominating factor with only two catches for 17 yards. The Commanders focused on the short passing game with seven completions to running

Jayden Daniels excelled on the ground in his debut, rushing for 88 yards and two touchdowns on 16 carries.

backs and another three to tight end Zach Ertz. It would take a while into the season for McLaurin to emerge once more as the team's top target, so he was patiently watching Daniels find his stride in the opener.

"I think [Daniels] showed great poise," McLaurin said. "He used his legs early when he had to. He gave us a chance on the outside. We just didn't quite connect like we wanted to. At the end, I just feel like he played really hard, he played strong. He's not afraid to put his head down and get the extra yards. He's not afraid of this."

An 0-1 start is a hard lesson, though not unfamiliar in Washington over recent decades. This season, it would be not how the Commanders started, but how they would finish that mattered more.

"We teach, and we get better," Quinn said. "This team is going to get a lot better. We're not going to be the same team tonight that we are down the line." ■

HE'S A SMOOTH OPERATOR

Jayden Daniels Exudes Cool and Calm, On and Off the Field

It was inevitable a nickname would fall upon Jayden Daniels. All great athletes receive them. But unlike many that come from teammates or fans, Daniels' friends and family named him "Smooth Operator."

"When I run, people say it doesn't even look like I'm running fast because everything just looks smooth," Daniels told "Boardroom" on YouTube. "I'm very smooth and everything I do out of structure, out of the ordinary. Not too many people are like me to do the things that I could do on the football field.

"Everybody's too different respectfully, but the main thing is like how I'm able to torque my body or be able to move around faster than other human beings at the size that I am. I mean, you don't see that from too many people, the unpredictability.

"I think that's the fun part in sports and just life in general. Being in this space. You gotta be comfortable being uncomfortable. You want to go out there and achieve the goals that you want, whether that's Super Bowls or stuff like that. You never know what's going to happen. You can start off the season 10-0 and lose the rest of the games, but I think you gotta be comfortable with just living in that space of 'Man, I'm going out there prepared for this moment. I prepared all week to go out there and be blessed to go out there and play on Sundays.'"

There are a lot of facets to Daniels. Like the hardest thing on the practice field is throwing the ball into a yellow trash can 30 yards away in the back of the end zone.

Ten weeks into the 2024 season, the rookie quarterback was already a leaguewide phenom. He led Washington to a 7-2 start in what would later be an NFC Championship game run. There were so many Offensive Player of the Week belts piling up in a box in his garage it was almost embarrassing.

But that yellow trash can humbled him. Friday practices included quarterbacks and even coaches floated the ball into the can. Daniels was nearly 0 for 60 attempts.

When Daniels finally completed the challenge, he yelled to nearby media over

The effortless running style of Jayden Daniels is the root of his nickname, "Smooth Operator".

COMMANDERS
WASHINGTON
5

OAKLEY

whether they filmed it. Funny how little things can mean so much.

"Something fun we have done with the QBs," Daniels said. "It is an intentional drill but also brings out the competitiveness among players and coaches."

People mostly know Daniels on the field. They don't know he's a funny, easy-going guy who's generous and superstitious. And, surprisingly, a bit of an introvert.

"I've never been the type of individual that I could say looks for fame," he said. "I am a very introverted individual, so I just go out there and live my life how I live it. I don't really go to too many places or I didn't before that so that isn't going to change for me either."

Daniels eats waffles only on game days for good luck, saying, "It's kind of like a superstitious thing. Something I've been doing since my freshman year of college. Shout out Bisquick."

Bisquick? Who gives a shout out to waffle mix?

Anyway, Daniels can be a chow hound. On Thanksgiving, macaroni and cheese is first on his plate. Yes, the food President Thomas Jefferson brought to America after discovering it while an ambassador to France (along with waffles and ice cream.)

Also on his holiday plate? Turkey, ham, mashed potatoes and gravy "but mac and cheese is No. 1 to me."

Meanwhile, the Commanders will play on Christmas in 2025, but Daniels remembers growing up always watching the NBA triple header each year soon after ripping open presents. Daniels is a big Los Angeles Lakers fan and rooted most for superstar Kobe Bryant.

As Santa, Daniels bought each of his offensive lineman an electric scooter, so they didn't have to walk so much. A physically battered unit, the gifts were much appreciated by the linemen.

Daniels occasionally attends other Washington sporting events. He wore an Alex Ovechkin jersey to a Washington Capitals game, was courtside for the Washington Wizards and Mystics and threw out the first pitch for the Washington Nationals.

You'd think a quarterback could throw a baseball with some oomph. Turns out it's a different skill set. His offering was a bit outside and nearly hit the plate, much to the amusement of many Commanders. Film of that throw was saved for a future team meeting that needed some levity.

Daniels' penchant for very early arrivals – probably around 5 a.m. like his college days though no one knows for sure since some coaches don't even arrive until at least 6 a.m. – forced the team to change the access entry codes. Players often don't show until 7 a.m.

Finally, Daniels cites legendary quarterbacks Tom Brady and Peyton Manning as role models more for what they do off the field.

"How they market themselves, how they carry themselves as franchise guys," Daniels said. "Hopefully, one day [I'll] be in their shoes. And you never see off-the-field issues about them. They carry themselves with a high standard and I want to be in their shoes one day. But I've got my own dream, my own role to take." ■

Jayden Daniels and his cool, calm personality is a good contrast to head coach Dan Quinn's fierier demeanor.

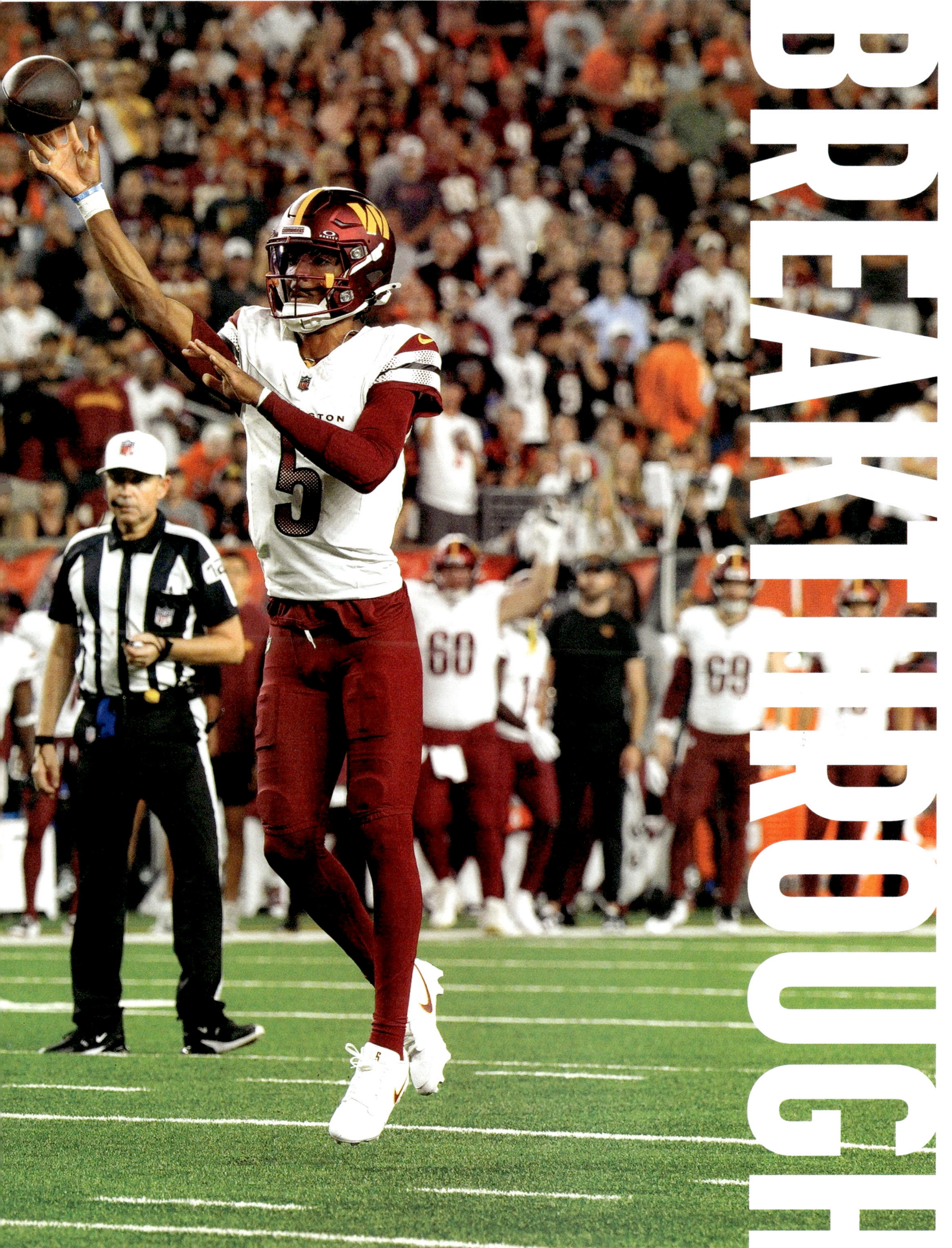

BREAKTHROUGH

A MONDAY NIGHT PARTY

Jayden Daniels Lights Up Bengals and Beats Fellow LSU Legend Joe Burrow on the Big Stage

This was the moment Jayden Daniels became one of the NFL's elite quarterbacks.

It was a Monday night party and Daniels was just getting started. An NFL rookie record for highest completion percentage that doubled as a franchise mark. Two touchdown throws and another running. And, that didn't include a 55-yard bomb that was perfection.

The Commanders took the Bengals apart 38-33. Daniels completed 21 of 23 passes for 254 yards and 141.7 pass rating. The 91.3 completion percentage was a Washington franchise record, too.

"[Daniels] is the answer, and we know he is," said Commanders defensive tackle Jon Allen.

It was the breakout expected from the second pick in the draft at an unexpected moment. Traveling to a desperate Cincinnati Bengals that were 0-2 despite labeled a Super Bowl contender, Washington instead provided its first peek into their own championship quest.

Ironically, coach Dan Quinn spent the week trying to temper players' excitement of being on Monday Night Football to his rookies.

"We recognize Monday Night Football – it's a lot of fun. It really is," he said. "And the environment's good. There's a stage on the field. It's a [lot] of people out on the field before the game. It's awesome. It's like just chaos and crazy.

"And so for most of the guys, I wanted them to enjoy the buildup for the game and then once it kicks off you go. But there is a buildup to go, and for [Daniels] and for the other rookies you go through firsts a lot.

"And if [Daniels] was somebody, like me, that was wanting to head butt the wall before you go out, I'd be nervous. But that's not him, you know? So, he has no D-line background in him. He's one cool customer."

Said Daniels: "Don't let a moment get too big or too little and go out there and silence the noise."

On the opposing sideline was Bengals passer Joe Burrow, whose shadow Daniels was always chasing at LSU. Burrow won a national title and Heisman Trophy in 2019. Four years later, Daniels won a Heisman, but LSU missed the national playoffs at 9-3 thanks to a poor Tigers defense.

Jayden Daniels and the Commanders were feeling good after winning a second game in a row, 38-33 over the Bengals.

COMMANDERS
OAKLEY
COMMANDERS
OAKLEY
NFL
WASHINGTON
5

JOHNSON
52

Burrow is No. 1 down in Baton Rouge, La. but Daniels is his own kind of legend. And now his role model had to concede after their first pro meeting.

"I'm watching [Daniels], he played great," Burrow said. "I told him that after the game. Congrats to him. Big time performance."

Not bad for a "nice college offense" as Bengals cornerback Cam Taylor-Britt called it. Washington scored on all seven possessions before a kneel down just like the previous week versus the New York Giants when kicking seven field goals. Tress Way didn't punt in either game.

There were so many special moments that night. With the Bengals making a fourth-quarter comeback, Washington found itself fourth-and four on the Bengals 39. Washington converted a fourth down in the first quarter. Daniels yelled "Let's go" to the sideline, though no one is sure whether he meant for the play call or converting a fourth down. It was a risky call because kicking a field goal would have extended Washington's lead to eight.

"I don't know. I was blacking out," said Daniels when asked which scenario he wanted. "I was focusing in the zone so I couldn't even tell you when I said that."

Daniels found tight end Zach Ertz for a nine-yard conversion. Three plays later, McLaurin scored on a 27-yard reception against zero coverage.

But it was the 55-yard catch earlier against double coverage by McLaurin that showed chemistry with Daniels. The first two games lacked that sizzle, but McLaurin urged Daniels to find him.

"[McLaurin] said, 'Trust me,' and that's what we did – trusted him," Daniels said.

Said Quinn: "It makes sense by giving those two a shot. They put the time in and if they hadn't put that time in, then you wouldn't have the confidence to throw into that space. Of all the work they've done, obviously they haven't connected on the deep points area in the first two games, but we knew that wasn't going to be the case moving forward, so when we had our chances with moments to go it took a really good throw and a really great catch from Terry."

Then there was Daniels' first career touchdown pass to offensive tackle Trent Scott of all people. Just offensive coordinator Kliff Kingsbury proving his mad scientist reputation with a one-yard toss that Scott practiced once weekly.

"Kliff called in the play kind of low on the shot clock," Daniels said, "so getting the guys set and going – and they were all discombobulated on defense – we got a sneaky one for Trent. It was awesome for him, and awesome for me."

Daniels needn't prove anything to teammates. They'd seen him daily since May make amazing throws in practice. Now a national TV audience knew the rookie was legit.

"Hey, that kid has poise," McLaurin said. "I think he grew up tonight. On that deep pass to me, that was a little bit of double coverage, and I've been pushing and pushing and pushing like trust me with that safety flat and give me enough air I can go get it. And for us to make that play,

Jayden Daniels showed off all the tools in the win over Cincinnati, going 21 of 23 for 254 yards and two touchdowns passing, as well as 39 yards and a touchdown rushing.

and for him to continue to make throws like that, use his feet to get first downs, the dude is tough, man, and he grew up tonight.

"He's been doing a great job in camp making those throws, but to come out here and do it when you've got to have it with the game on the line – that's what great players are about, and I think he's going to be well on his way if he continues to work."

Linebacker Bobby Wagner was becoming one of Daniels' closest friends despite facing each other in practice. Wagner watched Daniels keep making plays throughout the night realizing the newcomer could carry the team if the defense floundered.

"[Daniels] played amazing. Some of those throws were just on point," Wagner said. "I didn't realize he had only two incompletions – that's crazy. So, he's growing and gaining confidence, and you can see it."

Any second guessing that goes with being a high draft pick was gone. Daniels earned his credibility on that night in Cincinnati.

"A few days ago, I asked him what he learned in the first two games and it happened again tonight" said Quinn, "but as far as the competitor I've known that and as far as talent or arm, I've already known that, it was good to see the next step of him of when to take the shot and when not to. So, I did learn a lot more tonight and he's listening too and knowing the importance of that." ■

Fellow LSU legends and Heisman Trophy winners Joe Burrow and Jayden Daniels speak after the Commanders win over the Bengals.

RAVENS vs BENGALS
38
33

CAUSE FOR CONCERN

Washington Fans are All Too Familiar with an Injury Derailing a Promising Young QB

If there is one fear among Commanders fans over Jayden Daniels, it's injury.

In 2012, Robert Griffin III was like Daniels – a No. 2 overall pick after winning the Heisman Trophy. Both passers are blazing fast runners. Indeed, Griffin could have become an Olympic sprinter in 100- and 300-meter hurdles.

In his first month, Griffin scored on a 76-yard touchdown run that was the longest run by an NFL passer in 16 years. Griffin gained 138 yards against Minnesota that day and 815 yards overall plus seven touchdowns that season.

Griffin didn't know how to slide, didn't want to know, either. He could outrace defenders to the sidelines if needed. But after suffering a sprained knee late in the season, Griffin was badly hurt chasing an errant snap in the playoffs versus Seattle. He was never the same again.

Now Washington fans worried over another running quarterback with franchise-changing capabilities that could be lost in trying to do too much. Honestly, losing Daniels the same way Griffin exited would be crushing to fans.

Fans watched Daniels taunt defenders with his speed and agility, faking linebackers and safeties out with a quick move that too often turned inside instead of the sidelines. He carried 16 times for 88 yards and two touchdowns in the opener at Tampa Bay. Indeed, Daniels ran 16 or more times in four of the first six games.

"Some quarterbacks just really know how to do it. It's instinct," coach Dan Quinn said. "One, he has great speed and great acceleration, but he is also a really, really instinctive, talented runner. I would describe it as slashing. If you're indecisive, these guys are big and fast and they're going to get you."

Much of it was Daniels' playbook knowledge that let him know where blockers were positioned to protect him.

"Here comes the blitz to this side, get to the check, get to something else," Quinn said. "Knowing where to go with the correct read. At the end of it, it's just having command, honestly, whether it's in the huddle or at the line of scrimmage. This is a guy that has had a lot of

While the Commanders pummeled the Panthers, 40-7, Jayden Daniels had to leave the game early with an injury to his ribs.

NFL

COMMANDE
5

starts and a lot of experience. That showed up early for when he first started here."

Offensive coordinator Kliff Kingsbury didn't want to take away one of Daniels' strengths. Quarterback Marcus Mariota with a similar running style tutored Daniels over sliding. After all, Mariota is a master slider. But Daniels needed to be true to himself.

"You love the competitive nature," said Kingsbury of Daniels. "It just there's a time and place for it. He's played that way his entire life. He's very, very fast. He knows what he can get away with and what he can't. And then he also knows protections and knows when he should be picked up and when he is not. He can kind of set guys up."

The reckoning came Oct. 25 against the Carolina Panthers.

Washington led 10-0 after two possessions. He completed both of his passes while gaining 46 on one of his three runs for 50 yards overall. But Daniels landed awkwardly when hauled down from behind on the long run. He finished the drive but held his left ribs after plays.

Daniels then left the game and speculation went wild. The team clarified little over the injury trying to prevent opponents from knowing exactly where to hit Daniels.

There was never a recovery timetable for Daniels. He missed practice on Wednesday and Thursday before Chicago as Marcus Mariota readied to start. That almost always means a player is out on Sunday.

Daniels felt better on Friday and ran through drills on Saturday well enough for Quinn to let the former start if the passer warmed up well on Sunday. Let's just say Mariota's helmet was never far away during the game.

Daniels downplayed the injury and further padded the ribs. It was simply whether he could handle the pain. By game time, Daniels wasn't thinking about pain but winning the game with a Hail Mary that seemed further unlikely given his sore ribs.

Naturally, Daniels threw a 56-yard touchdown as time expired to beat Chicago.

"I admire so much about his California cool side to him," Quinn said. ■

Given the franchise's fraught history at the quarterback position and the career altering injury to Robert Griffin III, Washington fans were concerned to see star rookie Jayden Daniels exit the game against Carolina.

BELIEVE IN MIRACLES

A Legend is Born with Unforgettable Hail Mary to Stun Bears

Washington needed a miracle and received a Hail Mary. Suddenly, all things were possible.

The Commanders arrived at midseason 5-2, but a recent bruising loss to Baltimore and bruised ribs to Jayden Daniels the previous week left Washington a little anxious over the season's path.

A victory over the visiting Chicago Bears (4-2) before a national audience would confirm the Commanders were no longer underachievers. A loss, though, would invite doubt.

With the intensity of a late-season game, the highly anticipated matchup of No. 1 overall selection Caleb Williams and No. 2 Daniels became more of a defensive stalemate.

Washington gained a 12-0 lead, but Chicago ended the third quarter with a breakaway 56-yard touchdown. Then, the Bears sucked the life out of Northwest Stadium by scoring with 25 seconds left for a 15-12 lead.

A throwaway midseason game became one for the ages while Daniels ascended to legend.

Coach Dan Quinn wondered if the team had a next gear to improve and found the room wasn't too big for Daniels.

"He has continually during his time here to show early on to veterans 'Hey, is this guy gonna help us?'" coach Dan Quinn said. "You're constantly being put to the test to see how you'll respond. And so, he really earned that respect from his teammates."

On their own 24-yard line with 19 seconds left, the Commanders needed a big play for a possible tying field goal.

"I thought we'd had a chance if we could get up the field some," Quinn said. "That's what I was trying to get to. Could we get into field goal range if we could get a big chunk and get a timeout and then get a must out of bounds. So that's what I was hoping that we would accomplish into that spot."

First down was that needed big play, but Daniels missed Ertz downfield. Washington then made up 11 yards on a pass to Ertz. Five seconds left, Daniels completed a 13-yarder to McLaurin.

Jayden Daniels went 21 of 38 for 326 yards and an epic touchdown that will go down in NFL lore.

5
52
NIKE

TEVENSON
29
EST
19
COMM

The Commanders were still 52 yards away with two seconds left. It was too far for a field goal, so it was all up to a miracle throw.

Washington was ready to make its own miracle. The Commanders practice the Hail Mary each week. One man in front of the pile, one in the back. This time it was Noah Brown in the rear just in case there was a deflection.

Daniels nearly missed the game after suffering a rib injury the previous week versus Carolina. It wasn't until Saturday that Quinn was convinced Daniels could play. Now the coach was asking for a deep throw that requires body and soul.

Daniels took a seven-step drop and found nothing. It was too soon. He needed another few seconds for receivers to reach the goal line.

"Jayden did a fantastic job of buying time," Quinn said, "buying time over to the right side. I don't know how long the play was . . . but it took a long . . . time. Thirteen seconds? Yeah, I felt every bit of them."

The pass rush was nearing Daniels. He first went to the right, then crossed back to the left hash mark looking for a receiver.

"It's like a feel thing," Daniels said. "Kind of everybody's over huddled up waiting for the ball. It's kind of like a rebound after somebody shoots a long three.

"I was juiced up for sure. I'm excited because, I mean, that's kind of a once-in-a-lifetime experience."

The throw was more of a low-level line drive than a rainbow.

"I knew Jayden had the arm," said linebacker Bobby Wagner watching from the sidelines, "and all we had to do to was give him a chance."

The pile awaited the throw at the 2-yard line, which if even completed might have been finished short of the goal line with time expired. Three players gained a piece of it before the ball bounced high into the end zone.

"I thought the real factor was Zach Ertz," Quinn said, "going up to get a tip, to keep the ball alive and for Noah to get there. Because it's hard just to go up and snatch it so you almost have to go up and expect a balance or a tip to go.

The ball bounced right into the hands of Brown, a steady seven-year veteran acquired shortly before the season to be a tall No. 2 target. The Commanders often look first to Terry McLaurin in big moments, but Brown could be trusted.

It was Brown's only touchdown of the year. He would play just five more games before suffering a season-ending kidney injury.

"I'm not surprised at all by this happening," Brown said, "because I know we don't give up until the final whistle."

Washington won 18-15. The crowd of 64,704 went mad. The field saw one sideline racing to midfield in celebration, the other side slumped in frustration.

Chicago cornerback Tyrique Stevenson taunts Washington fans prior to blowing his defensive assignment in what would become one of the most memorable plays in franchise history.

"I felt a little like, rest in peace, [former N.C. State basketball coach] Jim Valvano," Quinn said, "just running around, not sure what to do or where to go."

It was Daniels' national moment where reputations are won or lost. Teammates had spent three months with him making plays in practices and games, so the walk-off win wasn't too surprising.

"The dog, that's the dog in him," running back Brian Robinson said. "We've known that he has it in him. He just showed us what he's capable of and how tough he is."

Defensive tackle Daron Payne had seen the Commanders lose many such final-snap games since drafted in the 2018 first round. Finally, it was his turn to walk away with the smile.

"Stuff usually does not come out on top for us," he said, "so just being able to be the ones that come out happy and celebrate with the guys felt good."

Turns out, it was just the beginning of Washington's late heroics. ■

Wide receiver Noah Brown hauls in a 52-yard Hail Mary touchdown pass from Jayden Daniels to stun the Bears and help spark the Commanders to an unforgettable season.

RIDING THE ROLLER COASTER

Jayden Daniels and the Young Commanders Learn the Highs and Lows of NFL Life

Jayden Daniels never lost two straight games in high school or college. Now he was mired in a three-game losing streak threatening to undermine the Commanders surprising 7-2 start.

And it bothered him . . . badly.

"I'm learning, you don't ride the roller coaster," he said. "You stay even keeled throughout it all because it's a long season. A lot of things can happen in a game in the NFL. I just try to stay even keeled and control things you can control."

It was a forgettable November. The Commanders lost a heartbreaker 28-27 to Pittsburgh Steelers. Four days later, they fell to the Philadelphia Eagles 26-18 in a Thursday night game. Now given a 10-day break, thoughts of returning fresh vanished in a 34-26 loss to the Dallas Cowboys when 31 combined points were scored in the final three-plus minutes.

Now Washington was 7-5 with second guesses ranging from opposing defenses figuring out Daniels to his hitting the rookie wall when college seasons typically end but the NFL is grinding towards postseason.

"I don't know if I ever had a two-game losing streak," Daniels said, "but I know its ups and downs, and you have to learn different things throughout the rookie year. Like I said at the beginning of the season, everything's not going to be perfect, even though I wanted to be perfect. But, you know, it just comes just playing the position, man. You have to go through some stuff. You have to go through adversity. It's how you respond. So, you know, I feel like we'll respond great, we'll rest up and we'll get back to it."

It's not like Washington was falling apart. Pittsburgh and Dallas could have easily been victories. The Steelers trailed most of the game before scoring with 2:22 remaining over a wilting Washington defense.

"There were moments and there were opportunities and so this one stings badly," coach Dan Quinn said.

Pittsburgh's secondary mixed coverages well and Daniels completed only 17 of 34 for 202 yards and a season's second-worst 68.5 pass rating. He only ran three times for five yards. The Steelers kept him pretty bottled up.

Washington's loss to Pittsburgh was the first of three in a row during a slide that was a good reminder of how tough it is to win in the NFL, particularly with a rookie quarterback in Jayden Daniels.

COMMANDERS

"Enjoy the process. Love the process. Learn to fall in love with it," Daniels said. "Wins and losses are going to happen in sports. Everybody can't be perfect. It's somebody's else's day that day. So just how can we go back and bounce back? How can the guys shift their attitude from a loss to a short week? How can we go out there and get better?

"I don't like losing so I don't want to feel like this. I don't want to have losses. I want to win in everything I step foot in and I put my mind to so I wouldn't say it's any motivation...When I win, I want to keep winning. When we lose, I don't want to lose. I want to win again."

Well, Washington lost on a short week as the NFC East-leading Eagles blew past the Commanders' 10-3 lead early in the third quarter with 23 unanswered points before Washington scored with 28 seconds left. Daniels was slightly better than versus Pittsburgh. He completed 18 of 28 for 221 yards, one touchdown, one interception and an 88.5 rating.

Yet, two losses in four days took some starch out of Washington.

"We knew that adversity would come," Quinn said. "It just does. That's our game. That's why we love it so much. There's hard parts, and tonight's hard. And, in fact, I even said that. The last two games were tough. They test your resolve, and they build some of your resilience. It's a difficult four or five game stretch, whatever it is. And it also emphasizes the ability to go close it, be there at the end and go win it."

Daniels conceded the team lost its offensive rhythm at midseason.

"We haven't been executing how we were before at the beginning half of the season," he said. "So, we've got to go back and, like I said, look at ourselves in the mirror. How can we get better? How can we keep improving? It's a long season, so there's going to be ups and downs, but how can we fight through adversity?

While the first two losses could be tempered with solid opponents, the third versus Dallas was perplexing. After a few days off, Washington faced visiting Dallas that was struggling.

The Cowboys went on a 17-0 run in the second half for a 20-9 lead. Daniels countered with a touchdown to Zach Ertz, but Dallas followed with a 99-yard touchdown return. Washington closed to 27-20 on a 51-yard field goal.

Things became even wilder. Terry McLaurin shook off defenders on a short pass to finish with an 86-yard touchdown for a 27-26 Commanders lead with 21 seconds remaining.

Would Washington pull off another last-second stunner? No, because Dallas again scored on a kickoff return.

Ecstatic to deflated in seven seconds. Washington blew a win.

"I told the team after the game was that this is the most challenged we've been in our time together," Quinn said. "I reminded them it's not enough to learn the lessons, but we have to apply them. Love the fight that we have, fight games, but we gotta apply them.

"To be the heavy hitters that we want to be, you've got to be able to close and be in those, but there's no moral victory side of things. It's just, how do you learn the lesson to close? How do you learn to do that? . . . You knew this adversity is coming. It just does. Every team's got it.

Jayden Daniels and the Commanders dropped to 7-5 with a loss to the division rival Cowboys but it would prove be their last misstep of the regular season.

Sometimes it's earlier, sometimes it's later."

Now the Commanders were searching for reasons of the downturn. Was a young team suddenly gassed with five weeks remaining? The "rookie wall" has been less of a problem in recent years after colleges expanded from 10 to 12 games plus reaching 15 games via playoffs.

"Usually in college the season's about to end," Daniels said. "Our season, it's just starting. That's different."

Offensive coordinator Kliff Kingsbury later felt team's Dec. 8 bye helped Daniels especially after a whirlwind offseason.

"That's a long stretch when you're talking about a guy who won the Heisman," Kingsbury said. "You go to all those functions and you go to the draft prep. I mean, you don't get a break. Just to catch your breath, week 14, and come back you can tell he's just rested, feeling better and hopefully that can lead to really good play down the stretch."

The drama soon stopped as Washington beat Tennessee to end the skid. Indeed, Washington won its last five regular-season games plus two postseason outings until falling in the NFC Championship.

It seems Quinn's lament of lessons learned finally arrived after three rough weeks. ■

JD AND BOBBY

Jayden Daniels and Bobby Wagner Bridge Generations, Sides of the Ball

Bobby Wagner was holding court with the media during a nondescript weekday presser when passerby Jayden Daniels cried, "Shut up."

And everybody laughed.

It seems the two are always jawing at each other in fun. Sometimes rapid fire, occasionally a dismissive missive. No one takes the words seriously.

"[Pressers are] what happens when you know how to read," Wagner retorted to Daniels. "We know you get own time, your own slot. . . Pull your pants up."

Daniels: "Bobby Wagner is so annoying."

They are sons of the Inland Empire of Southern California, a vast desert community once known for orange groves about 60 miles east of Los Angeles. Yet, they are distant relatives at best. Wagner is long deserving of a future Pro Football Hall of Fame selection as a banger of a linebacker. Daniels was entering his rookie year knowing of Wagner but not realizing how close the two would become.

"Me and Bobby, we're from the same area so we have that connection," Daniels said. "I didn't know Bobby at all. Never crossed paths before. I knew of him but didn't know him personally. Ever since I got here, we kind of just hit it off and he's like a big brother to me. Always giving game, taking care of us and I was cracking jokes, too."

The ongoing jokes are remindful of defensive linemen Kenard Lang and Dan "Big Daddy" Wilkinson when they were Washington teammates in the late 1990s. Lang was the 1997 first-round edge rusher who played next to Wilkinson, who arrived in 1998 as a pricey interior run stopper after selected first overall in the 1994 draft by Cincinnati.

Wilkinson was 300-plus pounds versus a sleeker Lang, who was 50 pounds lighter. Their lockers adjoining in the practice facility, Lang was often heard joking over Wilkinson's weight, saying, "Big Daddy is trying to lose weight. He's eating salads – potato salad, macaroni salad..."

Wilkinson would look up slightly with the vibe of someone's father saying don't make me

Bobby Wagner and Jayden Daniels forged an unexpected bond given their age difference and statuses on opposite sides of the ball.

NAGNER
54

FOX SPORTS

get up out of this chair.

Now, it's Daniels following Lang as the annoying little brother, always asking Wagner about defensive secrets. Was the passer tipping plays in practice, especially after seeing the linebacker adjust amid cadence during the opening days of 2024 training camp? That's the last thing a rookie wants to see.

"We're kind of talking about a check that I made and how [Wagner] knew when I made the check," Daniels said. "He already knew what was going to happen.

"I talk to [defensive players] all the time. Just what did they see? Why did they do this? What made you check to this? You try to soak up as much as possible and you got guys like Bobby that have been playing at a high level for a very long time. As much as I could be around them and pick their brain, you know I'm willing to do that."

It's not always about football. Wagner is one of the team elders, turning 34 shortly before the 2024 training camp. Daniels is a decade younger, which in locker rooms is more like a generation apart. That makes for a strange mix, especially when arguing over which rapper is better. And, there has been a standing invitation over which is the better basketball player.

"They do a lot of trash talking," said offensive coordinator Kliff Kingsbury, "but I think Jayden has great self-awareness, great situational awareness and he knows what greatness looks like. The level [Wagner] done it for so many years, how he carries himself, how he studies, how plays the game. That I know is a goal of Jayden's to be known as a guy who does it the right way on and off the field."

Daniels said Wagner's influence ranges from game preparedness to training table.

"Just how to be a pro," Daniels said. "How to take care of your body throughout a long season. How do you approach the game. How I watched film before week one and how I watch film now is completely different. I ask all the veterans how they watch film and break down stuff."

Punter Tress Way told SI.com that general manager Adam Peters should be credited for creating a roster chemistry that prevented an age-based pecking order that divides some locker rooms. The Commanders are all in on developing Daniels as their franchise cornerstone while Wagner's return for 2025 was uncertain until re-signing after the season.

"For Adam to vet those personalities and bring it together," Way said, "you had your biggest superstars on both sides of the ball, and they approach life basically the same way – with humility and a whole lot of contentment."

There are no friends on the practice field, but maybe that basketball contest will see some friendly bragging rights. The two never got around to it last season and most teams would prohibit it for fear of injury. Plus, whomever loses will hear about it every single day afterwards.

"One hundred percent – [Wagner] does annoy me," Daniels joked. ■

The light-hearted relationship between Jayden Daniels and Bobby Wagner as leaders of the offense and defense, respectively, proved to be infectious to the rest of the team.

FITS LIKE A GLOVE

Offensive Coordinator Kliff Kingsbury and Jayden Daniels Prove to Be a Match Made in Football Heaven

The worst mistake NFL teams make is trying to fit a square peg in a round hole. And, it happens every year.

NFL coaches relish rookie quarterbacks even if the passer doesn't fit their system. No matter, they tell themselves, the coach can change them.

The best lies are the ones we tell ourselves. Coach Norv Turner thought he could make Heath Shuler more of a pocket passer than runner in 1994 when mobile quarterbacks weren't so valued. Shuler couldn't make the transition.

Owner Dan Snyder wanted Robert Griffin in 2012, Shanahan wanted Kirk Cousins. When Griffin and Shanahan couldn't agree on an offensive scheme in their second year together, the passer became expendable. A very expensive pick costing Washington three first-rounders to move up became a bust.

So it was very important the first draft pick by new general manager Adam Peters fit what coach Dan Quinn wanted. And, what offensive coordinator Kliff Kingsbury was planning.

Within days, Daniels grasped the playbook. Within months, Daniels was knocking out late wins with ease.

And after one year, Kingsbury and Daniels look like they've been together for a decade.

The secret – they work together. You're thinking, "What kind of secret is that? Aren't they supposed to work together?"

Well, yes. But seldom do an offensive coordinator and rookie quarterback flow so effortlessly. Communication and hard work on each fueled an offense that proved unstoppable after midseason.

"I've always told those guys," said Kingsbury, "if you like [a play,] tell me. If you don't like it, tell me. I could think it's the best play in the world, [but] if you don't like it it's not going to work."

Normally, it's a little presumptive for a rookie quarterback to reject plays or provide negative feedback. That's a perk of a veteran star passer. But Kingsbury not only didn't mind but encouraged it.

"[Kingsbury] has a very quarterback friendly offense," Daniels said, "just for everybody in that

Offensive coordinator Kliff Kingsbury looks on during the early days of what would prove to be a fruitful partnership with Jayden Daniels.

OAKLEY
COMMANDERS
5
NFL

room to go out there and be able to learn it. It's not something you go out there you are worrying about what is this? What is that?"

Kingsbury understands quarterbacks, having spent the previous year turning Caleb Williams into a star at Southern Cal to earn the overall 2024 first pick; one ahead of Daniels. Kingsbury is a member of the Texas High School Football Hall of Fame after throwing 34 touchdowns to lead his team to the state semifinals. Kingsbury then set seven NCAA records and 39 school marks at Texas Tech while winning the Sammy Baugh Trophy as the nation's best college passer in 2002.

A sixth-round pick by New England in 2003, Kingsbury missed the team's Super Bowl championship season with an arm injury. Cut the next year, he spent the season on New Orleans practice squad. After two weeks with Denver's practice squad in 2005, Kingsbury later joined the New York Jets and even played later that season when completing one pass for 17 yards. After a stint in NFL Europe in 2006, he later spent part of training camp with Buffalo before sitting as a reserve in the CFL.

And that was it. Kingsbury turned to coaching with stints at three different Texas colleges before becoming a surprise hire as the Arizona Cardinals head coach at age 39 in 2019. Kingsbury went 28-37-1 with one playoff loss before being fired, but he resurrected quarterback Kyler Murray's career. After one season at USC, Kingsbury rejoined the NFL in Washington.

One thing that quickly sticks out when talking to Kingsbury – the wheels are turning behind those eyes despite looking straight at you. They're always turning as Kingsbury has a mad scientist reputation. He arrives daily around 4 a.m. despite working late nights, too.

Yet, Kingsbury is an unassuming soul, though seemingly bruised a little from his Arizona experience. Maybe he'll try head coaching again one day but he didn't seek Chicago's opening in early 2025 despite the chance to reunite with Williams.

Right now, Kingsbury wants to ramp up Daniels' game and is always open to suggestions. He often says good ideas know no rank and takes input from anyone. That's why Kingsbury is able to produce a different offense per passer.

"I would just say there's no one size fits all," he said. "You got to kind of figure out what makes them tick. What they like, what they don't like and how to best build your offense around them. And it's going to take a little while for us to figure that out completely."

Kingsbury marvels at Daniels' turnaround speed from first looks to mastery.

"Jayden's really good at processing information and letting you know, 'Hey, I felt comfortable with this, didn't feel comfortable with that,'" Kingsbury said. "And that's been really good for us as we've installed the offense, and

Jayden Daniels thrived in Kliff Kingsbury's dynamic offense during his rookie season, with plenty of opportunity for growth in the years to come.

we really try to pour it all on him and see how he could handle it and he's handled it well. But he's not afraid to let you know if a concept [is something] he doesn't like or familiar with. And that's really been a good relationship."

Kingsbury noticed Daniels' ability to continually grow even before Washington drafted the latter. The 2025 offense will certainly change from the passer's first season via an offseason reboot. Nobody's expecting a sophomore slump by Daniels.

"What I liked most probably about the college tape was just the drastic improvement you saw year in, year out," Kingsbury said. "That shows the guy's putting in the work and studying and doing those things you have to do to try and be great.

"[Jayden's] intentional in everything he does, which I like. That's what we heard about him coming up and that's what he has been since he's been here. He has been focused, intentional and got to work." ■

PRACTICE MAKES PERFECT

Preparation Pays Off as Commanders Knock Off Eagles in Thriller

The Commanders won a game in practice.

Ten seconds remaining against the Philadelphia Eagles in a late-season, must-win game. The Eagles split coverage with two high safeties. The linebacker didn't follow Jamison Crowder into the middle of the end zone. Jayden Daniels spotted the coverage break and threw his fifth touchdown of the game with six seconds left.

Washington 36, Philadelphia 33.

"We hit that in practice," Daniels said. "That's the same exact concept, same exact throw so it was kind of just like I see two high safety, middle field open and I already hit this in practice, so it was time to make the same throw and end the game."

By now, a late victory was becoming classic Daniels. With the confidence of "Cool Hand Luke" that defined 1960s movies, there was no failure to communicate by the Commanders leader. After throwing a devasting interception, his second in a season of only nine picks, that led to Philadelphia's 33-28 lead, Daniels and the Commanders regained possession with 1:58 left now needing a touchdown to win.

"[Daniels] doesn't change at all on that stuff," said offensive coordinator Kliff Kingsbury. "You could just tell from the look in his eye if we get the ball back, we're going to win it. And that was like his feel. That [interception] one of the most brazen throws he's probably made. And I think he was just trying to make a play. He can rest and there was no like, 'Oh, we lost the game' or 'That's on me.' He was like 'All right, if we get the ball back, I'm going to win it.' And that's what the sideline felt and his teammates felt and his coaches felt."

Working exclusively in shotgun formation needing 57 yards to win, Daniels threw three short passes to three different receivers before running 12 yards to the Eagles 23 with 44 seconds left. After another short pass for seven yards to Terry McLaurin, Daniels again took off for two yards.

The Commanders now worked the clock with Brian Robinson running five yards to the 9 before Daniels spiked the ball to stop time with 11 seconds left. Crowder, who barely played all season because of injuries, caught his second touchdown of the day to beat the Eagles.

A strong week of practice and well executed game plan helped Jayden Daniels and the Commanders knock off the rival Eagles.

COMMANDERS
19
COMMANDERS
5
19

"I love those types of situations," Daniels said. "It's on thin ice and plays need to be made. That's what you live for if you really love this sport. You play for those big-time moments where it comes down to the end. Until the end, everything's against you, your backs against the wall – how will you respond?

"I always believe we can win a game no matter what. The game is never over until the clock strikes zero."

Said coach Dan Quinn: "If you give him his moments, he really lights up in those spots."

By now, last-second comebacks were becoming standard. Kingsbury joked of getting shorter haircuts to hide his increasing gray temples. The Commanders would later reach the NFC Championship thanks to a series of Daniels winning rallies at games' end.

"There's a lot more under the hood for us," pledged Quinn.

Daniels finished with a career-high five touchdowns. He completed 24 of 39 passes for 258 yards and a 99.1 pass rating despite two interceptions. He also gained 81 yards on nine carries. Overall, Daniels carried the team on an afternoon when the Commanders couldn't stop Eagles running back Saquon Barkley's 150 yards and two scores.

"Today, [Daniels] became a heavy hitter. Honestly, all the way back to Week 2 is when I first learned it," Quinn said. "We were playing the [New York] Giants. We were behind going into a two-minute [drill.] It was in that moment. [Daniels said,] 'We got it, Q.' And it was the same one today. He made a fourth and 11 scramble and

Jayden Daniels made a big impact on the ground in the win over the Eagles with nine carries for 81 yards.

COMMANDERS
93

got down to the field. I said, 'This is it. You stay in this moment. You stay where you're at.' And, he stays consistently level."

The Eagles blew off the loss, blaming the loss of quarterback Jalen Hurts on a scramble just five minutes into the game when hit by linebacker Bobby Wagner. Uh, sure.

This victory was a statement win for Washington after beating a series of mediocre teams. The Eagles would win the NFC East and the Super Bowl. Indeed, the Commanders were the last team to beat the Eagles in 2024. Washington wouldn't lose again until the NFC Championship to Philadelphia."

"I think this was a toughness game," Quinn said. "Today was an example of resilience and connection as a team...This is living in the NFL. It isn't going to be good [all the time.] There's going to be tough deals and bad moments and you stay in the fight and keep going."

Dallas has been the historic rival of Washington since the 1960s, but Philadelphia runs a close second. "We want Cowboys" has become a cliched chant by older fans. The next generation wants a piece of the Eagles.

"Beating [Philadelphia] was really fun," Wagner said, "and I think for our fans and for everybody that's been through a lot the last few years – I haven't been here for all of them, but I've heard – to be on this side of it and to be moving in the right direction for everybody to see the direction this team is going, I think is special." ■

Jayden Daniels let it fly early and often against the Eagles, going 24 of 39 for 258 yards, five touchdowns and two interceptions in the key win.

COMMANDERS
COMMANDERS
5
NFL
NFL

THE FINAL WORD

Commanders End Playoff Drought with Clutch Overtime Win Over Falcons

Washington coach Dan Quinn loves to talk of playing five quarters to demonstrate grinding hard to the end. To clinch a playoff berth, the Commanders really did have to play five quarters with Jayden Daniels getting the final word.

The Atlanta Falcons needed a victory to reach the postseason. Washington probably didn't, but why take chances? So, both teams landed haymakers. Trailing 7-0, Atlanta delivered a 17-0 run before halftime. Then Washington returned for 17-0 streak only to see the Falcons awaken to tie the game with 79 seconds remaining.

This time, Daniels would wait for overtime to deliver his patented late victory.

Washington won the coin toss and never gave Atlanta a chance. The 13-play drive used only one run for one yard. The rest was on Daniels, who ran five times himself. Daniels was mostly in sync with tight end Zach Ertz. After two short passes, Daniels found Ertz in the end zone for a two-yard touchdown.

Washington 30, Atlanta 24. The Commanders were going to the playoffs for the first time since 2020 while the Falcons were out.

The team seemed more relieved over not letting down the crowd of 64,128 that roared through the second half, smelling playoffs for only the sixth time since 1993. The unexpected postseason following 4-13 in 2023 seemed magical and everyone inside Northwest Stadium relished the moment.

"The fan base waited a long time for this," Daniels said. "I really can't put into words how much it means to them and how much it means to me to be able to go out there and lead this franchise and lead this team to opportunities like that."

Coach Dan Quinn cited the crowd as a critical factor for a team that was "gassed."

"The first thing I want to acknowledge is the fans and feeling their energy tonight for five quarters," he said. "Man, we felt every bit of it and they really deserve a cool win like that. For

Jayden Daniels had a career day on the ground in the win over the Falcons, rushing 16 times for 127 yards.

COMMANDERS
5

COMMANDERS
COMMANDERS
5

us to have that connection with them, they're as big a part of it as you can imagine when you're feeling it on the sideline...I really thought this was a great demonstration of their connection [with fans.]"

Said special teamer Jeremy Reaves, who proposed to his girlfriend on the sideline after the game: "It's December football. Like these are winning time moments. DQ preaches all the time, winning time moments. Everything equates to a winning time moment. The energy, it's infectious. Good or bad, it can play a role."

The near constant close games all season saw Washington again rally through Daniels. It seemed the Commanders were just expecting to eventually win.

"It's nights like tonight that you do gain a lot and it's tough and it's grimy at times and you have to overcome things," Quinn said. "But those are the times that we get to learn.

"They've become a little hardened and knowing that they're not out of the fight. I felt that shift take place against Philadelphia...We're into those fights and know that stay in it, stay in it, say in it.

"It got hard. It got behind. And over the last couple of weeks there's been some moments like that, and they coined the term 'Our Time,' meaning...that's a focus for that moment. And one of the things I admire so much about that is they're never out of the fight. I love coaching these guys, what they stand for...We got a lot more under the good and a lot more to fight for. And so, no time for us to be nostalgic and that. We've got work to get done."

Aside from Brian Robinson's single carry, Daniels was instrumental in every overtime play. He opened overtime with a seven-yard run, threw to Ertz for 10 and ran again for seven before Robinson's run. Daniels then ran for 16 yards, passed to Ertz for four, then Chris Rodriguez for 12 and Robinson for four.

Daniels ran for eight yards to the Falcons' eight before stuffed for no gain. Backup quarterback Marcus Mariota told Daniels, "Stand up, catch your air, get your wind and go out there and execute. Use your God-given abilities and let's win this game."

The moment wasn't too big for Daniels, saying, "It's a lot of ups and down and adversity in this game that you go through and you go through in life. You never waver, you stand tall, stand 10 feet down and go out there and try to execute the moment."

Daniels scrambled six more yards to the two-yard line. Now Washington had Atlanta on its heels and finished with a familiar play the Commanders ran regularly in practice.

"Man coverage. I knew they were going to keep eyes on Terry [McLaurin] and I knew Zach had one-on-one," Daniels said. "We repped that so many times I knew [Ertz] was going to win on

The Falcons had little answer for Jayden Daniels, as he went 24 of 36 for 227 yards, with two touchdowns and an interception.

that. He was going to make the catch and it was going to be game over."

Said Ertz: "Jayden threw that ball about 1,000 miles per hour. He was saying I was going to catch that ball, or no one was going to catch it."

Just how was Daniels able to keep winning walk-off games as a rookie? Even his coaches were amazed.

"[Daniels is as] good as I've ever been around as just playing the next play," offensive coordinator Kliff Kingsbury said. "He doesn't let much phase him. He knows the work he's put in during the week and he focuses on that. He can process it and move forward. And for a young guy to be able to handle that with all he has going on has been impressive."

Quinn said the competitor in Daniels is just unequaled.

"He is a dangerous player and not by design that some of these runs took place when it's the time comes to go," Quinn said. "We knew we were going to be bold. But at the end of the second half especially, there was just some strong plays and he just willed it. That's the competitor he is."

The playoff slot now secured, Washington would largely let Daniels rest in the second half of in the finale versus Dallas to ready for the playoffs. ■

By dispatching the Falcons, Jayden Daniels and the Commanders clinched a playoff berth for the first time since 2020.

THE BIG PAYBACK

Commanders Take Down Rival Cowboys as Jayden Daniels Gets a Break and Mentor Marcus Mariota Thrives

Can it really be a good season for the Commanders without beating the Dallas Cowboys?

The Commanders weren't ready to finish their best regular season since 1991 just yet. They'd deliver one last walk-off win, only this time someone else threw the pass while Jayden Daniels celebrated.

Coach Dan Quinn rested Daniels after a lackluster first half, sensing the latter's sore legs were bothering him more than the passer admitted. Instead, Marcus Mariota learned moments before leaving the locker room that he'd finish the game.

Mariota wasn't wasting a rare moment on the field. He rallied Washington from a 9-3 deficit midway through the third quarter with a touchdown pass to Zach Ertz. The teams traded scores three times with Mariota scoring on a five-yard run.

But Dallas led 19-16 in the waning moments. It looks like a series sweep for the Cowboys until Mariota followed Daniels' penchant for last-second wins with a five-yard touchdown pass to Terry McLaurin with three ticks remaining.

Commanders 23-19.

Daniels normally shows little excitement over wins, but this time he was howling in glee for his friend.

"I'm so happy for [Mariota] and everything he's been through in his career," he said. "He didn't have to take me under his wing. He's done that, plus more. I'm so happy for him to go out there and have a game like this. A game-winning drive, last play, go out there and walk it off.

"I love this team. I love how everybody approaches their week of preparation and next man up mentality. You can see it out there in Marcus."

It was Mariota playing the cool veteran role after the win this time.

"We wanted to just kind of continue this momentum going into the postseason and our guys fought hard all day," Mariota said. "That's kind of been the nature of our team throughout the year. We have a collective of group of guys who just believe in one another, regardless of

While Jayden Daniels played limited snaps in the season ending win over the Cowboys, it was still a nice cap on the season to avenge the November loss to the NFC East rival.

OAKLEY
NFL

COMMANDERS
WASHINGTO

what your role is. Anybody can come in and make plays."

The leg soreness appeared hours before the game. Daniels said he would have played the second half if it was a must-win.

"100% - they would have to drag me off the field," Daniels said. "Just some leg soreness. It plays a part. Other than that, it is just the open communication that we have and ultimately DQ made the decision, so I respect it."

Daniels conceded he was all in for Mariota during that winning drive.

"Selfishly, I want to be a part of that," Daniels said. "But obviously, just to see those guys and see how Terry just broke the franchise record with a walk-off touchdown and Marcus, everything he has been through in his life and in his professional career."

Washington finished with four straight walk-off wins; dagger-like efforts that would continue into the postseason. The winning year was so unexpected the series of heart-stopping victories didn't even earn national attention. There were no "Cardiac Kids" or so nicknames because fans and media outside Washington didn't realize what it was truly seeing.

"We've got a flair for the dramatic," McLaurin said. "That's for sure. I think it's a testament to our team to be resilient and fight through those. We never know how it's going to show up. I think we all know that we could be better in the first quarter, first half and get a little more rhythm for our team and play more complimentary football. When we do that, I feel like we can move the ball confidently."

It would be good training for the postseason. The season was a whirlwind to Daniels as it is for most rookies. So many adjustments to a longer schedule, steady travel, heavy media demands and more kept Daniels from even thinking about the playoffs until now.

"I don't know what the playoffs feel like, so I will find out next week," he said. "Obviously, everything is going to be amped up. It's one and go home. You don't have another week. I think it is more amped up based on the outside noise."

Ironically, the second season would begin like the first – at Tampa Bay. ■

With a playoff spot already clinched for the Commanders, it was an easy decision to give Jayden Daniels the second half off in the win over the Cowboys.

'WE JUST HIT IT OFF'

Washington Football Legend Doug Williams and Jayden Daniels Build a Friendship for the Ages

Most mornings at Commanders Park, Jayden Daniels and Doug Williams share a few moments before the day's work becomes non-stop.

The Most Valuable Player of Super Bowl XXII who's now a Commanders senior advisor and the 2024 NFL Offensive Rookie of the Year aren't talking football. They're discussing the game of life where a young man asks an elder how to handle challenges off the field.

"[Daniels] doesn't need another coach. He has a bunch of coaches," Williams said. "I talk to Jayden on what's going on with him and his family. Stuff like that. That means more to him than me telling him about a player."

It is a close relationship dating back to 2019. Daniels was a freshman at Arizona State where Williams was delivering a seminar over challenges for Black quarterbacks. The two clicked so well that Williams met Daniels' parents and keeps in touch with the family regularly.

"[Williams] is someone that has been through it and someone that I can lean on whenever," Daniels said. "Doug has always been great. Just helps me with things and is someone I am really comfortable with. All of his advice resonates."

The bottom line on the relationship – they simply like and respect each other.

"[Daniels] is always who he is – an engaging person," Williams said. "We just hit it off. How well he plays the game of football, he's a better human being.

"Part of that is his personality. If you watch Jayden no matter the situation, what has happened, what's going to happen – his demeanor does not change. The good, bad or ugly, he's not getting in anyone's face. His demeanor never really changes."

Daniels admires Williams' past accomplishments. A 1978 first-rounder by Tampa Bay, Williams played five years with the Bucs, jumped to the USFL for two years and then spent four with Washington where he won the Super Bowl in his second season.

After retiring as a player, Williams then coached with four colleges and NFL Europe

An icon among Washington football fans, Doug Williams has forged a unique connection with Jayden Daniels.

before becoming Grambling State's head coach. After scouting for 15 years for Jacksonville and Tampa Bay and two years as a United Football League general manager, Williams returned to Washington in 2017 serving various roles. That wide-ranging resume is why Daniels is always willing to listen no matter the subject.

"The history man, that man sitting back over in the corner, Doug Williams," Daniels said. "First Black quarterback to win the Super Bowl. To be able to lean on [Williams] and how they have success here and maneuvered throughout this organization, I'm open ears for sure. I'm ready to learn."

The relationship is well known throughout the building. Past team legends weren't around the training facility often during owner Dan Snyder's tenure of 1999-2023. Williams-Daniels' friendship is one the Commanders hope sparks more.

"They're very connected and it's nice for both of them to see this relationship grow," coach Dan Quinn said. "Whether it's a quarterback or being in this community...Doug has a special lens for that."

Beating Cincinnati on Monday Night Football in week 3 was Daniels' national coming-out party. It was a preview of a season filled with winning big games. Daniels saw Williams in the tunnel afterwards to celebrate together.

"It was awesome," Daniels said. "Obviously, it was a very emotional, hard-fought win on the road in a hostile environment...Doug was doing

Legendary head coach Joe Gibbs and former quarterback Doug Williams both maintain a presence with the Commanders.

this back in his time and he put in the time here. It meant a lot."

Williams tried to mentor past Washington rookie quarterbacks like Robert Griffin and Dwayne Haskins. Neither player was interested. But Williams knew Daniels was worth mentoring.

"When I saw [Daniels] and [teammates] Bobby Wagner and Zach Ertz form the best relationship you want to see a rookie make, I watched that," Williams said. "I saw it happen. Most guys who are second in the draft, they make a lot of money, play quarterback, their mindset is not there. Jayden knew who he was. He knows what he's accomplished. He treats people like people ought to be treated."

Williams said Daniels most reminds him of former quarterback Alex Smith among past Washington passers. Both quarterbacks handled teammates well.

"As far as engaging, his people skills," said Williams of the pair's commonality. "As far as teammates, they have the same demeanor."

Williams conceded his relationship with Daniels is a source of pride.

"It's a good feeling when a young guy looks at you from that standpoint," he said. ■

The MVP of Super Bowl XXII, Doug Williams reached the top of the sport, an accomplishment that Jayden Daniels hopes to replicate.

REDSKINS

A LESSON IN LEADERSHIP

Commanders Construct a Team of Leaders to Help Jayden Daniels Reach Potential

The master class that was the Commanders coaching and front office one-year franchise turnaround was best shown through leadership.

General manager Adam Peters and coach Dan Quinn didn't want to overload rookie quarterback Jayden Daniels. Quarterbacks are assumed to be team leaders, but it's often asking too much for a rookie.

Peters and Quinn devised a plan to let Daniels grow into the role by gathering other leadership candidates. With the roster only keeping 40 percent of players from the previous year – the team's lowest since 1945 – the Commanders signed linebacker Bobby Wagner, tight end Zach Ertz and quarterback Marcus Mariota to be leaders and role models.

The trio were all 10-plus year vets. Wagner and Ertz are probably Pro Football Hall of Famers on their first ballot. Mariota became Daniels' mentor while leading in early practices and quarterback room sessions.

Meanwhile, Peters drafted seven players who were their college team captains. The rookies quickly integrated on a team that was much like a new franchise where nearly everyone in the building was new thanks to a massive clean sweep.

None of this normally happens. Newcomers sit back in locker rooms for their first year while letting established team leaders run the team. However, Washington was largely short on carryover leaders with receiver Terry McLaurin the sole one.

Wagner and Ertz weren't afraid to take over; indeed, they relished it. With college newcomers ready to join, the team adapted well to challenges right from the start when Quinn introduced a footwork drill to begin practices. It was a lot of yelling, screaming and heart-pumping moments that created adrenalin flowing for better workouts.

"I think you got leaders all over the locker room," Daniels said. "Guys that step up respectfully and they're each in their position.

Former Pro Bowl tight end Zach Ertz was one of many veteran leaders that the Commanders brought in to help in the development of Jayden Daniels.

So you just come in, kind of just be yourself and that's how I do, that's how I take my approaches to go out there and be myself. I don't have to be nobody else who I'm not. DQ tells me that all the time – just be you. That's gonna be enough. Those things come in time. What you need to do is absolutely deliver on your end."

Other leaders provided Daniels the luxury of time to worry about himself rather than shouldering the team. That would come soon enough.

"You don't have to put the cape on and carry the team," said Quinn to Daniels midway through preseason. "All I want you to focus on is playing quarterback to the very best of your ability...You can just lock in and do your thing... Nothing where he had to take on a leadership mantle that he didn't need to yet. That'll come."

It came on a Hail Mary to beat Chicago on Oct. 27.

The Commanders' 12-0 lead was suddenly a 15-12 deficit with 25 seconds remaining. Washington tried to get upfield quickly for a potential field goal but was still 52 yards away with two seconds left.

As always, Daniels was stone cold on the final snap. After crossing the field twice evading defenders and sore ribs that limited his deep game, Daniels launched a Hail Mary that found Noah Brown all alone.

Touchdown. Game over. The first of five walk-off wins over the season.

"There's a lot of resilience in this guy," Quinn said, "that has always been there. I don't think any of us will ever forget the finish of tonight. It was really cool."

Said Daniels: "I didn't see anything. I just heard people screaming on our side, rushing the field. So that's how I knew."

It was a watershed moment for Washington. Now 6-2, it knew tough losses to eventual playoff teams Tampa Bay and Baltimore meant the Commanders were better than recent years, but not sure things for the postseason yet.

Beating a comparable team in Chicago showed Washington's penchant for close losses over many years could be reversed. And, that new confidence showed up weekly later in the season. After losing three straight to sink to 7-5, the Commanders replicated their walk-off magic versus Chicago by winning the last four games – all on the last play.

The Hail Mary showed teammates Daniels could win games. His confidence was infectious as the defense just figured keep it close and give Daniels enough time to win.

In a midfield postgame meeting after defeating Atlanta to clinch a playoff berth, Quinn told Falcons coach Raheem Morris, "There's some things that five [Daniels] does that you can't put on a card."

Daniels demeanor always impresses

Marcus Mariota's mentorship was vital in the early stages of the career progression of Jayden Daniels.

teammates. He's the same win or lose, midweek or game day. If the team needs a comeback, he delivers a "no problem" approach, grabs his helmet and heads to the field to deliver.

"You see him on the bench," Ertz said, "whether it's right before the two-minute drill and overtime, he is literally just the same person. Whether it was OTAs when we're working the two-minute drill against the defense or with the opportunity to go to the playoffs and solidify ourselves with an opportunity to go to the playoffs.

"He's the most mature rookie I've ever been around. He approaches the game, he loves to learn. And so, he exudes a quiet confidence. He's not out there, a rah-rah guy, but we all know how good he is and how much confidence we have in him. And so, he doesn't need to say anything."

Each week, Quinn chose different game captains for offense, defense and special teams to reward everyone's hard work. But come the playoffs, Quinn knew who to pick for the duration

Daniels was a postseason game captain. ■

THE DOINK HEARD ROUND THE NFL

Jayden Daniels and Commanders Capture First Playoff Win Since 2006

The Commanders' victory margins were now so close it was almost comical when beating Tampa Bay on a doinked field goal.

"I felt like I was in a Bounty commercial where the cup spills. And, like, 'Nooooo!'" said coach Dan Quinn. "And as it hit and went through, I just paused and probably skipped a beat, but that's the emotion where it was at. We put it on the left [hash mark] and was thankful to knock it through. But it was definitely a long 8-9 second field goal."

Washington survived the Tampa Bay Buccaneers 23-20 in the first round of the NFC playoffs as time expired. Zane Gonzalez's 37-yard field goal hit the right upright the width of a dollar bill and bounced through the goal posts.

In a season of walk-off wins, that was a miracle.

"I can't really explain it," said Jayden Daniels, who became the fourth NFL rookie passer to win 13 games. "Obviously, I'm grateful to have the opportunity. I'm happy for the fan base, the franchise, everything it's been through to get to this point. I'll just say I'm grateful and happy for everybody, including myself, too.

Washington was steering toward the first-round game since a 7-2 start. Still, Quinn became the first Washington coach since Dutch Bergman in 1943 to win a playoff game in his first season with the franchise. Not Joe Gibbs, Ray Flaherty or George Allen, who all reached championship finals. Instead, it was Quinn with a dedicated one game at a time mentality.

"Maybe it's the volume of close games you've been in," Quinn said. "I've been on teams that were exceptional, but they were maybe not in a lot of close ones. So, when that becomes the norm, I think you live in that moment more often. And I think that is probably what has taken place with this group. They have a lot of belief in one another.

"Jayden certainly is a big factor in that. I think if he had his heart rate monitor on, and mine, they would not be the same in the game.

In his NFL playoff debut, Jayden Daniels went 24 of 35 for 268 yards and two touchdowns in the win.

WASHINGTON
5

RIDE SHARE
ROUTE UPDATE
INNOVATION
BUCS
WASHINGTON
5

His stays pretty consistently good."

Said linebacker Bobby Wagner: "I think it's the camaraderie, I think it's the brotherhood. I feel like we've been tested throughout the year. We had moments where we were up, we had moment where we were down and I think all those tests have allowed us to build that confidence especially for a group that's first playing together, especially for young players that we have that are playing really big minutes so all these wins are good for our experience and makes it fun for us."

Washington built a 10-3 lead with Daniels tossing a 10-yard touchdown to Dyami Brown before Tampa Bay tied it with 10 second remaining in the first half. The teams traded leads three times with Daniels finding McLaurin on a five-yard score early in the fourth quarter for a 20-17 edge.

"Terry wasn't necessarily one-on-one," Daniels said, "but he had a corner outside leverage, who had the safety inside leverage to take away anything. I was able to check some, and Terry made the play.

"I think you just kind of find that zone. And you don't hear [anything.] You just focus on your fundamentals, and you focus on playing in the playoffs."

Daniels was no longer a rookie come playoff time. That conversion happened in midseason and honed to a point in December. He wasn't afraid to carry the offense. Daniels didn't often ask offensive coordinator Kliff Kingsbury to let him do so, but JD could when needed.

"I guess you can say what's understood doesn't need to be explained," Daniels said. "But I know Kliff has the utmost confidence in me. I know the team does. I know they have the utmost confidence in him and the guys to go out there and make plays. That's why I distribute the ball out to the guys, and they go out there and make plays.

After Tampa Bay tied the game at 20-20 with 4:41 remaining, Washington never gave the ball back. A deep 21-yarder to Brown on third down saved the drive nearing the two-minute timeout.

Austin Ekeler later took a pass 18 yards, then ran for 8 more as Washington reached Tampa Bay's 19-yard line with nearly one minute remaining. Daniels converted another third down with a short pass.

With Tampa Bay later out of timeouts, Daniels kneeled at the Bucs 19 after letting the clock reach three seconds before using Washington's final timeout. Gonzales then made his trick shot and Washington was on to Detroit for the NFC semifinals.

"This is what we've been doing all season," McLaurin said. "This is what [Daniels] has been doing all season. It's the preparation that we put in and I know people may be tired of hearing 'winning time moments,' but that's real and it shows up and I think that is what the playoffs are

Jayden Daniels made more history with the Commanders, helping the franchise secure the first playoff win since 2006.

GONZALEZ
47
WAY
10
WASHINGTON
69
27

about. You may not play the perfect game, but if you have the ball to go down there and have a chance to win the game, we trust our preparation in the moments we've been in this year.

"And to see Jayden [Daniels] continue to just get us in the right calls, execute what Kliff [Kingsbury] is calling, showing some poise, just taking complete command of the game, complete command of the huddle, is – I'm fortunate to play with him and see how much he's grown this year but that's who he is."

Wagner was also not surprised to see the team win its fifth straight walk-off game.

"[Jayden's] done it all year," Wagner said. "We understand it's the playoffs, but it's still the same game. That's kind of what we've been preaching all week. Obviously, the stakes are a little different, but he came in and played the game that we know he's capable of playing and did a great job. ■

The Commanders swarm kicker Zane Gonzalez after he doinked in the last of his three field goals in the historic win.

DOMINATION IN DETROIT

Commanders Stun Top Seeded Lions, Vault Jayden Daniels to Elite Status

A magical season was supposed to end in Detroit. Nobody told the Commanders.

In its best game of the season, 8½-point underdog Washington eliminated top-seeded Detroit Lions 45-31. Jayden Daniels was in the middle of it all again, throwing for two touchdowns and 299 yards with a gaudy 122.9 pass ratings plus another 51 yards on 16 carries to lead a rushing attack with 182 yards and three touchdowns.

"Surreal moment just for the Washington fanbase – whole DMV," Daniels said. "It's just an awesome feeling."

Washington advanced to the NFC Championship versus the Philadelphia Eagles. It was one more victory away from its first Super Bowl appearance since 1991 when earning its third Lombardi Trophy in eight years to end a 20-year run of the franchise's greatest era. This time, a team many figured would win six games just took its 14th in convincing fashion over the Lions that dominated the regular season at 15-2 for the NFC's top seed.

"I always believed that we could achieve more than what people give us credit for," Daniels said, "but you've got to go out there, put in the work. You've got to go out there and work daily, get better each and every day and just put your head down and grind, and by this time in the season, you look up and you might be in a position like this."

Washington was in this position because of Daniels, though he would never say that. But the truth is the defense was average at best, the running game often disappeared and the battered offensive line sometimes cratered.

Yet, Daniels had the knack of making others better, partly through his running capability to buy time for late wins like the Hail Mary versus Chicago. Partly because his passes were seldom inaccurate. But mostly because he just refused to surrender.

"[Daniels] just has a different poise about him than most and he's a rare competitor," coach Dan Quinn said. "There's no doubt about that. But in those moments…if he was a basketball

Jayden Daniels and the Commanders went on the road to Detroit and shocked the NFL by knocking off the heavily favored Lions.

WASHINGTON
5

player, he'd want the last shot. As a ball player, he wants the ball in his hands to make the difference and he makes great decisions with the football and that takes real mindfulness. Sometimes the best play may be, 'Hey, I have to throw this away.' He uses his legs, but he is a rare competitor for us. But his poise in these tight moments really stands out to us."

Daniels' boyhood idol was Kobe Bryant of the Los Angeles Lakers. Using a trick by childhood friend and 2023 first-round passer C.J. Stroud, Daniels often warms up before practices and games using a basketball that gives him a better grip when downsizing to a football. He can just grip and rip.

Daniels definitely wants the last shot. Ironically, this was the first game since Thanksgiving that he didn't need to win at the end.

It was Washington's best game of the season. Detroit's pass rush was neutralized by Daniels' aggressive film study. This game was a prime example of why the passer analyses defenses so much. He knew the Lions plan and adjusted.

"Know where your man-beaters are," he said, "beat man-to-man coverage, and we did that."

Daniels found Terry McLaurin for a 58-yard touchdown midway through the second quarter that put the Commanders ahead for good. He later followed with a five-yard scoring pass to Zach Ertz for a 10-point edge shortly before halftime.

Jayden Daniels continued to look like a veteran on the playoff stage with 299 yards and two touchdowns through the air.

CHOOSE LOVE
SMITH
5

WASHINGTON

Ertz and McLaurin were prime targets all season and Daniels wasn't forgetting them now. The passer threw nearly 60 percent of his passes while drifting to the right side out of shot gun but could also tuck the ball. Gaining 51 yards on 16 carries with a 15-yarder meant most plays barely dented the Lions run defense but often set up Washington for another big play.

It felt like a déjà vu moment because the last time either team made the NFC Championship was Washington beating Detroit in the 1991 final. Now, Washington upped its playoff record to 4-0 over Detroit.

Washington would move on to the conference final against old rival Philadelphia, whom the Commanders just beat a month earlier. Still, there was no overconfidence versus the Philadelphia, just a moment of joy to defeat Detroit.

After all, Washington always had a puncher's chance with Daniels and he just KO'd Detroit. ■

With the shocking win over the Lions, the Commanders clinched a spot in the NFC Championship for the first time since 1991.

END OF THE ROAD

Commanders Put Up a Fight Early Before Falling to Eventual Super Bowl Champ Eagles

It didn't take long for the Commanders to put the NFC Championship loss behind them.

A glorious season ended with a 55-23 beating by rival Philadelphia Eagles. No ifs ands or buts, this was a beatdown.

Maybe that's easier because losing a close game to miss the Super Bowl is agonizing. It's something that takes weeks or months, maybe even a season to truly end mind games of what if.

Instead, Washington simply lost to a better team that would go on to win the Super Bowl. The Eagles pulled away shortly before halftime and then again when the Commanders closed within 34-23 with 5:01 left in the third quarter on Jayden Daniels' 10-yard touchdown run. Philadelphia scored the last three touchdowns for a lopsided score for the history books that really wasn't misleading.

"Man, it sucks. Man, it just sucks," Daniels said. "Excuse my language, but I couldn't be prouder of the guys in the locker room. You know, just year one, everybody not really knowing each other, rookies, the vets did a tremendous job of bringing us in and helping us out. And we all just meshed. And we got to this point, but at the end of the day, man, we lost. It sucks, but we'll move on from this.

"I don't want to have a feeling like this again. But you have to deal with it. You know, move on from it."

It's not that the game was too big for Washington after decades of mediocrity. The first-year roster under new coach Dan Quinn rallied after losing three consecutive games at midseason to win five straight on the last play and then routed NFC frontrunner Detroit in the divisional round. They deserved to reach the NFC Championship that was only a game away from the unlikeliest of Super Bowl appearances.

"They had enough discipline to stay in it for the wild card game," Quinn said. "In the Divisional week, they weren't thinking down the road. That was the same thing this week. It was just this game against Philadelphia, and that takes discipline when the outside world is like, 'Hey, you're two wins away.' So, yep, it's Philadelphia and so this was not a case of that. I want to make sure I'm super clear on that, so that is something to take away.

The biggest stage short of the Super Bowl provided Jayden Daniels a good learning experience about what it takes to reach the highest level in the NFL.

COMMANDERS
WASHINGTON
5
NFL

WASHINGTON

"Can you be disciplined enough to stay in the moment of the game? We did a good job on that during the season as well, where we just felt like we were never out of the fight. Those are important things to have."

Daniels was finishing his rookie season, but the passer was involved in plenty of major college games. That beating Philadelphia was the stepping stone to the Super Bowl didn't intimidate him

"It's just another game for me," he said. "That's how I treated it. That's how I treat every game. You have to go out there and earn it. You have to prove it. Tonight, we didn't earn it."

Daniels finished 29 of 48 for 255 yards, one touchdown, one interception and a 72.9 pass rating plus six runs for 48 yards and one score. Playing from behind took away the running game and the Eagles pass rush with three sacks provided little time for Daniels to look deep. Indeed, he threw 16 times to tight end Zach Ertz versus 21 throws towards receivers.

"It just doesn't seem like there's going to be one [game] that's too big, honestly," Quinn said. "[Daniels] has rare competitiveness that makes him unique in a lot of ways. I love inside how he can stay into this space in the toughest environments. It hurt him to come out at the end. He wanted to stay in. I said that's my call. But that's the competitor. Honestly, he's just kind of wired in that way."

Losing three fumbles plus an interception ultimate cost Washington its chance, especially after rallying in the second half.

"We kind of talked at the half. This is going to be grimy. We're going to fight back into it," Quinn said. "But that's the life that we've kind of lived this season. So we were comfortable in those tight spots. So we thought, okay, it's about to turn. It's about to turn. Then they got their takeaway during that next one."

Said Daniels: "Turnovers played a huge factor in a game, especially playing a good team like Philly. You can't give those guys extra possessions."

The postgame locker room was more of grim smiles of appreciation of a good season tempered by falling just short.

"No locker room is the same year to year," Quinn said, "and so I wanted to make sure they spent that time together because they've created something that's very cool here. It's going to pay off for years to come. Every person had a role in that.

"Sometimes, you end up on the wrong side of it, and you fight your way back. I do love that there's a lot of guys here, honestly, that are like, just down to get down when those happen, and they really want to fight together."

Daniels exited the season knowing it was just the start of the franchise reboot. It was the foundation of what he hopes will grow regardless of falling short in the conference final.

"Man, just the culture that Dan Quinn] and [general manager] Adam [Peters] set here.," Daniels said. "We know the standard. And locker room next year, we're obviously going to have new guys come in and stuff like that. So, we have to teach them the standard and uphold it to that." ■

The Commanders ran into a buzzsaw in the eventual Super Bowl champion Eagles, but they hung in the game long enough to find positives going into the off season.

BROWN
2
12

THE NEXT LEVEL

A SLEEPING GIANT AWAKES

After Downtrodden Decades, Winning Football is Back in Washington

The nation's capital is once more a football-centric town.

"The amount of passion the fan base has had has been incredible," said offensive coordinator Kliff Kingsburg during the playoffs. "I had not been around that where it's just live or die and really longing to be relevant again. And, you can feel it's tangible."

It wasn't always so. RFK was the nation's first multi-sport stadium, but baseball's Senators were the primary team over the Redskins. Basketball was the street game where neighborhood showdowns often drew 500-plus fans ringing the courts while college powers Maryland and Georgetown drew full houses.

Football's heyday was 1937-42 when the Redskins relocated from Boston to win two championships, but even its band was considered the bigger attraction. Indeed, halftime shows with 100-plus piece marching band was the reason many fans came.

Legendary coach Vince Lombardi arrived in 1969 and, in his only season before dying, led the Redskins to a winning 7-5-2 mark. The Senators left three years later to create a sports vacuum right when coach George Allen began his streak of seven straight playoff seasons and one Super Bowl appearance.

While the Baltimore Bullets and Washington Capitals arrived in the early 1970s, Washington was now clearly all about football. And when coach Joe Gibbs delivered three Super Bowl crowns from 1983-91, the Redskins dominated water cooler conversations across town. It became the one thing in a politically divided city that everyone supported.

President Richard Nixon once submitted a play (that failed miserably and cost a game.) Owner Jack Kent Cooke's box was considered the ultimate VIP ticket in town. Playwright Larry King was a fixture. Vice president Al Gore, Virginia Gov. Doug Wilder and U.S. Treasury Secretary James Baker came to games. Many politicians from across the country became Redskins fans since Capitol Hill was only blocks from the stadium.

Jayden Daniels was instrumental in bringing the Commanders back to relevance in a big way in the 2024-25 season.

OAKLEY
COMMANDERS
NFL
COMMANDERS
NFL

McLAURIN
17
FOOTBALL
5
28

Cooke died in 1997 and months later the team relocated to Landover, Md. where a stadium with 15,000 more seats was filled with fans often waiting a decade or more to buy season tickets. Owner Dan Snyder increased seating another 20,000 after buying the team in 1999 and still it was filled at 91,000.

The only problem – the team mostly stunk from 2000 to 2023 with a 4-13 mark in the final year. For years, fans often streamed out the exits at halftime of lopsided losses with only a few thousand left by game's end. That is, unless the opposing team's fans dominated the stands and stayed to relish the victory.

By 2023, that supposed 200,000 ticket waiting list Snyder often claimed was actually gone. Indeed, there were only about 8,000 season ticket holders. Maybe 5,000 of those fans came regularly.

Fan desperately wanted Snyder to sell amid two years of scandalous charges of front office misconduct against women staffers and cheerleaders. Lawsuits flew, the House of Representatives held hearings and the NFL obviously spiked one investigation before accepting results from an independent group upon Snyder's departure.

An economic fan boycott worked, especially when voters called their politicians to spike potential stadium deals in Virginia and Washington. Snyder was costing fellow NFL owners big money and the latter forced the sale despite Snyder's reluctance right up to the final hours before completing the record $6.05 billion deal.

The honeymoon was delayed six months as owner Josh Harris and Co. bought the team on the eve of the 2023 season. Too late to make changes, they readied for 2024 while the team lost its last eight games in a 4-13 year.

Harris then made a series of successful moves, hiring general manager Adam Peters and coach Dan Quinn, who knew they were taking a passer with the No. 2 overall selection. It didn't take long to focus on Jayden Daniels.

That one selection has made Washington football great again.

The unexpected 12-5 season, its best in 33 years, didn't stumble come playoffs. Washington won two postseason road games as underdogs to find itself in the NFC Championship.

One game away from the Super Bowl after a 4-13 season was mind blowing. Fans were a little reluctant to believe such fortune could come after a quarter century of misfortune. But the stands were largely dominated by Commanders fans throughout the season and the players and coaches felt that energy.

"You know what it meant? Honestly, so much," Quinn said. "We absolutely felt that. And I think from a home game perspective it was Atlanta for whatever reason.

"We were losing I believe at the half [17-

Safety Jeremy Chin shared the euphoria with Washington fans in the aftermath of the Week 8 Hail Mary win over Chicago, one of the most unforgettable plays in franchise history.

7] and to hear that crowd erupt, feeling the support behind them, you can't help but to win. And then see burgundy and gold [fans] down in Dallas and then in Tampa and smidgens of it in Detroit and again [at Philadelphia] we feel it. And we know how important football is to this community. To know that we're part of that, man, it's really awesome."

Beating Atlanta 30-24 in overtime courtesy of another Daniels rally clinched a playoff bid in the season's final home game. It was remindful of the old RFK days when old portable baseball bleachers at midfield shook up and down.

After three decades, the bandwagon was back.

"I had the best seat in the house," Quinn said. "I had a 360-degree view of it all and it was really cool to see. To feel the energy, that part of the third down, some false starts that went along with that and some offsides. That was absolutely caused by the crowd noise. So when we talk about a home-field advantage that's what we're talking about...I could hear them. I could feel them."

Suddenly, Washington football was great again. ■

Head coach Dan Quinn and Jayden Daniels hit the ground running in their partnership in Washington, with sights on bigger things ahead.

DANIELS
5
WASHINGTON
COMMANDERS

GATEWAY TO THE FUTURE

With Jayden Daniels, Anything is Possible – Including a New Stadium

It will be The House that Jayden Built.

Washington's expected new stadium in 2030 needed a winner to gain congressional approval for a lease extension. It needed someone to give fans hope. And, it will one day need a winning team to make fans pay higher ticket prices in the new venue.

Jayden Daniels wears the cape.

In coming years when the decade-long quest to replace Northwest Stadium with a mind-blowing near $4 trillion stadium hosting 200 other events aside Commanders games is built, it all comes down to Daniels.

Losing teams don't get mega-stadiums. They're stuck in old venues.

But Daniels is hopefully the face of the franchise for another decade or more so he'll see that opening day when everyone looks up to marvel at what money can buy. The rest of his current teammates? Well, maybe a few. The NFL stands for Not For Long when it comes to careers.

But whenever Commanders owners or Washington's politicians need someone to bang the drum for money, they'll show clips of Daniels making plays. Touchdowns. Victories. Maybe another Lombardi Trophy.

And that's when people open wallets to come to a new stadium even if parking is limited for little tailgating and personal seat license costs freeze out middle-class fans that supported this franchise since 1937.

No matter – Washington loves winners. It supports "events." Daniels checks both boxes.

Daniels succeeds Alex Ovechkin as the town's must-see player. And, Ovechkin could be seen 40 times annually with the Washington Capitals while Daniels has 10 home games at most. So, you gotta be there.

What will the new venue be like? The team is still working on renderings, but the old moat idea encircling the stadium that past owner Dan Snyder floated isn't happening. The old curved dome of RFK that turned summertime humidity into a sauna inside the venue will be replaced with a translucent roof. There may be a glass-enclosed west end zone. It will have a hall-of-

Jayden Daniels exceeded expectations in his rookie season on the field and may even help provide the momentum needed for a new stadium in Washington.

fame area for fans to wander through (probably on their way to the gift shop.)

There will be 65,000 seats, though another 5,000 can be temporarily added to reach the minimum to host the Super Bowl.

It's expected to have five floors where RFK and Northwest Stadium offered three. The vertical climb will make Northwest seem flat.

And that's it. Details are still coming.

But none of this happens without Daniels. Oh, it probably would happen without the passer, but it's sort of like America doesn't win its independence without George Washington. Oh, the U.S. would have probably followed Canada's path to freedom once day, but not anytime near 1776. And maybe the Commanders would have built eventually even without Daniels, but the path became a lot easier with him.

So forget the No. 5 jersey. Daniels dons the crown and cape as the Commanders forge to a new future home. ■

Jayden Daniels may not yet be on the level of legendary quarterbacks Joe Montana and Dan Marino, but his rookie campaign certainly put him on the right path.

FANATICS FEST
Fanatics
FANATICS
Fanatics
PASSING TIME

THE SKY'S THE LIMIT

Jayden Daniels and Commanders Get Back to Work with Lofty Goals Ahead

Barely two months after losing the 2024 NFC Championship game and weeks before 2025 OTAs and minicamp practices, Jayden Daniels was asked what he was doing.

"I'm sitting down and watching film and trying to eliminate some tendencies, as much as possible," Daniels told Yahoo Sports. "Talking to the coaching staff on areas that they feel like I need to improve on and having conversations so we can all hit at full speed."

What offseason?

Winning never takes a break and Washington's quest to reach the Super Bowl after falling one game short in Daniels' rookie season started just days following the playoff loss.

General manager Adam Peters attended Senior Bowl practices for a glimpse of potential draft picks. Then he traded picks to acquire left tackle Laremy Tunsil and receiver Deebo Samuel. Come draft time, Peters used the first rounder on offensive tackle Josh Conerly.

Translation: the offensive line was rebuilt with two new tackles and former tackle Brandon Coleman moving to guard to protect Daniels while giving him a second target behind Terry McLaurin.

Meanwhile, the running backs were kept intact and tight end Zach Ertz was re-signed along with linebacker Bobby Wagner, who takes pressure off Daniels as team leader.

So, the offseason really centered around Daniels while leaving the passer to just be himself. And, he's doing just that by hanging out at Commanders Park watching film like some career movie reviewer looking for clues in whodunit mysteries while also slightly bulking up.

"I gotta go out there and prove myself each and every day," Daniels said, "no matter if it was last season, this season, 10, 20 years down the road, you have to prove yourself each and every season. Outside noise doesn't matter, have to go there and keep proving yourself."

Offensive coordinator Kliff Kingsbury isn't concerned over force feeding more offense to Daniels. It will come naturally.

"Organically, it's going to happen as you continue to work with each other," Kingsbury

The work began anew for Jayden Daniels and the Commanders at minicamp in June 2025 leading up to one of the most anticipated seasons in franchise history.

5

COMMANDERS

said, "and [Daniels] continues to figure out his game and this offense and match the offense... He's not thinking as much, he's playing fast and letting his natural gifts kind of take over and that's what we want to see. So, I expect him to take a big jump."

Said Quinn: "There is no flinch in Jayden Daniels. He's an absolute like, as focused and relentless as you could about getting better."

But it wasn't easy to let go of that surprising and satisfying 2024 season when the Commanders shocked the world by rising to nearly the top after a generation of mediocrity. Quinn proved reflective in the team's final meeting.

"I wanted them to...savor this time," Quinn said. "They've created something special together as teammates. And not every locker room is the same year to year and knowing that next year's team will be different. But what they created I didn't want them to miss that because having great team chemistry is a part of a championship run. They know exactly what that looks like."

Chemistry helped Washington surpass expectations. Now they would reform. Eight free quickly signed elsewhere and many would not remain in Ashburn. Peters' plan is to rely on short-term free agents while the base is built through the draft. That means the churn recreates the roster annually.

"I think every year's different and every team's different," Quinn said. "Every team starts again at the bottom. Once this season's over we're 0-0 and every single day we're just going to try to get better."

When the Commanders returned in May to ready for Quinn's second season, Quinn promised some new looks.

"There's a lot of playbook that people haven't seen," he said, "featuring some new players and some into some different spots. I think Kliff is excellent at that. That's what's kind of fun about now exploring some new thoughts, some new ideas and some scheme while like sharpening on the things like can I go from really good at something to elite and to the best at this concept, this type of play, this footwork."

Indeed, Washington seems to have finally hit a lasting reboot after years of mediocrity.

"I don't even think about the past anymore to be honest," receiver Terry McLaurin said. "I'm living in the present, looking forward to the future." ■

Jayden Daniels knows that you must prove it again each year in the NFL to reach superstar status and win a Super Bowl ring, something not accomplished in Washington since 1991.

COMMANDERS
OAKLEY
OAKLEY
NFL
WASHINGTON
5